International acclaim for
Ordinary People Extraordinary Planet
by Dr. Shellie Hipsky

"People around the world will benefit from reading *Ordinary People Extraordinary Planet* because they will become enlightened while gaining a new perspective on life."
- Pu Ying, President of the *Erie Chinese Journal*

"Heartfelt and inspiring . . . a real page-turner."
- Jacqueline Aluotto, Award-Winning Filmmaker/Activist

"A great inspirational read. An opportunity to embrace and learn from the enlightening experiences of others!"
- Eleesha, Publisher, *Inspirational Authors and Writers Daily*

"This extraordinary book will empower you to help others while making your dreams come true!"
- Karen Hoyos, Global Transformational Leader/ Speaker/ Author and the Goodwill Ambassador to Bulgaria

"The people in this remarkable book learn from hard experience . . . they triumph because of their incredible determination and will. Cherish this book. Learn from it how to live and survive the times that are the toughest."
- David Evanier, Aga Kahn Fiction Prize winner and author of eight books such as *All the Things You Are: The Life of Tony Bennett*

"Courageous stories of overcoming adversity and building resilience. Today, our planet overflows with the love and inspiration that these remarkable people bring by sharing what they have lived and experienced. Dr. Shellie Hipsky and Ray Leonard cascade these parables as gifts from their hearts to yours."
- Maria Berdusco, President of Leadership International and Author of *How to Think Like a Leader*

Ordinary People
Extraordinary Planet

Ordinary People
Extraordinary Planet

Dr. Shellie Hipsky

Ordinary People™
Extraordinary Planet

KMR-MEDIA PUBLICATIONS
Grand Rapids, MI • kmr-media.com

Library of Congress Cataloging-in-Publication Data

Copyright © 2011 KMR-Media Publications

Distributed worldwide by KMR-Media Publications

Library of Congress Catalog Card Information on file with the publisher
Paperback ISBN-10: 0-9838699-0-1   ISBN-13: 9780983869900
Hardback ISBN-10: 0-9838699-1-X   ISBN-13: 9780983869917

Cover Design by Kathy Moody
Edited by Cori Nicole Smith
Authored by Dr. Shellie Hipsky
Based on Ray Leonard's Radio Show
"Ordinary People Extraordinary Planet"

Printed in the United States of America

Published by KMR-Media Publications
Grand Rapids, MI

Dedications

Dr. Shellie Hipsky's:
For my beautiful children, Alyssa and Jacob,
my husband, Joe,
and my parents, Libby and Jack Jacobs.
You all inspire me daily!

Ray Leonard's:
For Esmerelda, baby Gabi,
my brother Ron,
Dad Leonard, Mom Leonard,
Dad Cadena, and Mom Cadena.
Thank you for loving me in your own special way!

In Memoriam:
For our dear Clarel Radicella,
We thank you for your openness and inspiration!
You are eternally our beautiful angel with a purpose.

Contents

Acknowledgements

T hank you to the listeners in over 75 countries who support the Ordinary People Extraordinary Planet radio show hosted by Ray Leonard and to the amazing guests who he has befriended and skillfully interviewed. Thanks also to the courageous people who opened up to Dr. Shellie Hipsky while they provided insights for this book regarding how they became such inspirational people.

Cori Nicole Smith did a wonderful job as the editor of this book. Aubrey DiVito, Carrie Ferris, Sabine Cherenfant, and Susan Perich helped with the details of the project. Stefania Vitale, Fan-Yu Lin, Xiaobo LaPresta, and Queeney Tang are working to take this book global through translation into multiple languages. Nurses John Jacobs and Jennifer Herford provided medical terminology clarification when required. Chris Gribschaw, Dr. Chris Davis, and Dr. John F. Jacobs served as technical support. Kathy Moody's cover art provides a great visual representation of the words inside the book. Libby Jacobs served as a guide and magnificent support system during the writing of this book, as well as Shellie Hipsky's previous four books and over 100 articles.

Robert Morris University's dedicated leaders and faculty supported us in the writing of this book. Thank you also to Kathy Coder the President of Inta-Great and Dr. Claudia Armani-Bavaro an author and a leader of a corporate mentoring Program for a Fortune Global 500 Company for helping to create the OPEP Reading Guide for small groups, organizations, and book clubs.

Ray would like to thank Culligan of Grand Rapids, Lamont Primus, Jeff and Sandy Kaat, Les Lancer, Rob Sawall, Tavis Polinskey, Paul Spiketts, Billie Sue Berends, Beorn Bricka, Eric Nelski, and Jason Craner. Thank you to KMR-Media Publications, who published our book to reach out and inspire the world!

Foreword

Ray Leonard,
Radio Personality
Founder of KMR-Media

Photo credit: Esmerelda Leonard

What do you think of when you hear the words "broadcast studio"? Shiny microphones? Glass partitions separating you from outside noise? Sound technicians with their fingers hovering over the on-air mixing board? My very first radio broadcast studio was in a closet at home! Honest. It's pretty crazy the way I got into radio.

My beautiful wife and best friend, Esmerelda, is a pediatrician with a thriving practice. I had been working an office job I enjoyed when, one day, I was shocked to learn that my boss and mentor of six years had shot himself in our office. I was stunned that this exemplary man had killed himself. My wife, realizing how upset I was, said, "You know, Papi, you may want to take a week off of work." When I returned, the place where I worked was carrying on with a business-as-usual attitude. I thought, "It shouldn't be business-as-usual. A good man just took his life. Life is precious."

I decided to leave the company; I went back to school for a degree in communication. While I didn't take any radio broadcasting classes during my schooling, I always had a passion for talking. After graduation, I got a job as Director of Public Relations for Culligan. I worked with the owner of a broadcast company to develop two-minute segments about water for the radio. Because it was too short a show to produce in the studio, I bought a $23 microphone, which sounded like crap, and some computer software that wasn't very good, and from my closet at home, I called in to the station. I talked about topics related to water. I didn't focus on Culligan. Instead, I got into the stories from the environmental side — which you will read more about in Chapter Six with journalist Tasha Eichensher from National Geographic — and about water treatment. As the station gave us more time for our segment, we interviewed Good Housekeeping's Research Director Miriam Arond, congressmen in D.C. about the 1972 Water Act, and other experts.

After a great interview with "Jungle Jack" Hanna, I told my wife that the radio show is, "about something much bigger than just water." After all, you can only go so far with one subject, and I needed to broaden the topics — explore the human dynamic. I wanted to know what real people had to say.

Jack Hanna's interview revealed that he had grown up on a Tennessee farm, was fascinated with animals, and became a zoologist. He went on to teach the world about animals on his Emmy-award-winning *Jack Hanna's Into the Wild* and on short segments on shows such as *The Late Show with David Letterman*, *The Ellen DeGeneres Show*, and *Larry King Live*. The stories we captured during his interview inspired me to learn more about people and share their stories with my listeners.

I told Ez, "This planet of ours is really extraordinary." From there, I realized that no matter how big a deal you are – from a sports star to a Grammy/Emmy-Award-winning artist like trumpeter Arturo Sandoval who escaped Communist Cuba, whose story is told in this book – everyone is ordinary in some way. And the opposite is the same. After all, your own next-door neighbor could have conquered an obstacle and is doing something cool to help others. I wanted to find out what people were doing out there in this extraordinary world of ours!

With the help of Culligan, I began KMR-Media Network. A lot of people thought, "This dude is crazy. He is thinking and dreaming too big. I hope he doesn't flop." My wife reminded me how much I hate to lose or be told "no." Yet, Esmerelda declared that I could do this. She believed in me.

I found Roy Jaurez, Jr. who is featured in the first chapter. He was doing the Homeless by Choice Tour, reaching out to 100,000 students with his message, and was featured in the best-selling *Chicken Soup for the Soul* series and on CNN. His story of being homeless at 14 with his siblings resonated with my audience, and I was able to get him on television to talk about it and into the schools to spread his message.

When I was called into the office by the bosses at the radio station, I put on my game face as they asked my intentions for the program. They liked what I had planned and they changed my format to a half-hour show. While I was elated by this beginning for KMR-Media, we were soon celebrating another precious beginning in our personal life. As you hold this book or e-reader, I hold another labor of love in my own arms. On March 28, 2010, Esmerelda and I welcomed Gabriella Veronica Leonard, 19 inches and 7 pounds 9 ounces, into our lives. Now we had an even more important reason to make the world a better place by spreading inspiring stories.

Ordinary People Extraordinary Planet is now heard in 75 countries, including the United Kingdom, Mexico, and Saudi Arabia. The kmr-media.com website has gotten over a million hits.

The website now includes a thought-provoking blog by Tiffany Kennard, a young lady who is an over ten-year survivor of brain cancer who achieved her goal of getting her master's degree in occupational therapy to help others. Visit kmr-media.com and learn from her survivor perspective. People around the world are being inspired by the stories of my show's amazing guests like Tiffany. Despite life's ups and downs, her sense of humor and intelligence shine through in her words.

Sometimes fates seem to align with my guests and my mission to spread these positive stories. For instance, I interviewed Associate Professor Dr. Shellie Hipsky and her co-author Dr. Claudia Armani-Bavaro about their book *Mentoring Magic: Pick the Card for Your Success*. Shellie inquired if anyone had thought about writing a book about the people on the show. I was deeply honored when this respected public speaker and scholar said, "When you do, I would love to be the author!"

Now you are holding in your hands the results of all that hard work: the *Ordinary People Extraordinary Planet* book! We know that the stories inside will inspire and uplift you. You may also want to keep the Kleenex handy.

Stories like the one of our dear friend, Clarel Radicella, a terminally ill single mother and educator, who entrusted us with three moving letters to her dear children, will touch your heart.

Be prepared to go on a journey with this book. From the North Pole in Chapter Nine to the White House in Chapter Ten, there are people to get to know and places to learn about.

Also, please take note of the wonderful charities that each of our "ordinary" heroes have chosen to spotlight. Remember this proverb, "If you have much, give of your wealth. If you have little, give of your heart." Millions of people are helped by these charities. We are committed to helping them fundraise and spread awareness for their important causes. Let's continue to explore the extraordinary things we can accomplish together!

Ordinary People™
Extraordinary Planet

Chapter 1

Roy Juarez, Jr.

Photo credit: Tiffany Turk Photography

Ordinary People Extraordinary Planet

ROY JUAREZ, JR.

Roy Juarez, Jr., is a 30-year-old motivational speaker and the President/Founder of America's Business Leaders. He recently appeared on CNN with his mentor in a segment leading up to *Latinos in America*. Roy's compelling story has been told in the *New York Times* bestselling *Chicken Soup for the Soul* series. This is Roy now. But what made him "Homeless by Choice"? His story includes being homeless at 14 years old, rejected by adults, and forced to take care of himself and his younger brother and sister.

It all began when I was a 12-year-old living in San Antonio, Texas. My parents always had a rocky relationship and domestic violence was an almost daily occurrence in my home. Young as I was, my mother and I caught my father having an affair. For the next few months, I watched my parents' relationship boomerang: my mom would want my dad out, and he would come back; she would leave him again, and he would come back, and they would get back together. This pattern—so common in households with domestic violence—is hard to break without a good support system. Finally, after about a year of going back and forth, my mom decided that enough was enough and she wanted a divorce. But my father had different plans: "If I can't have you, no one is going have you!"

Violence and fear drove our family into hiding. We were constantly moving from home, to home, to home. Every time my dad found us, we had to pack up that night and move, again.

My mother turned to her family and friends for help and shelter, but it was hard for her to find places to live, especially with five children. It reached the point where we all had to go our separate ways just to survive. Looking back, maybe another way could have worked, but when you are in the middle of the storm, it's hard to see beyond it.

Many people ask me how a mother can do that to her own children and how a 14-year-old, 9-year-old, and 2-year-old could become homeless. The truth is, it happens more often than people like to admit. I have worked with students across the

2

country in 37 states, and I have discovered that my childhood situation was not uncommon.

In 2010, I launched the "MyBag, MyHome: Homeless by Choice Tour" — a 300-city tour across the continental United States with a goal to inspire 100,000 youth to dream, not give up on life, and understand the value of a higher education. While I toured across the country, I reflected on my past experiences and hoped I could use the lessons that I learned from the streets to help other youth. Every time I went into a school or I worked with teachers and service providers, I talked about my experience of homelessness, abandonment, and my struggles in education.

Homelessness was the great influence of my childhood, but the true story isn't encompassed by an isolated moment in time. In order to fully understand the turning point, you must understand the entire journey.

I began learning the lessons that would influence my life at seven years old. My dad had promised me a fishing trip, and I was so excited and couldn't wait for it to come. When the day finally arrived, I was playing with my cousins in the front yard of my aunt's house. My uncles and dad were busy loading the boat. It was almost time for us to go fishing! My dad called for me, said he was going to buy a bag of ice for the ice chest, and told me to wait for him on the front porch. As a child, I didn't think much of it when my uncles, cousins, and dad jumped in the truck and drove away. I trusted that my dad was telling me the truth. They didn't come back for two days, and when I realized what happened, I learned a harsh lesson about life. At seven years old, I learned how to be angry, hateful, and distrusting and how to hold a grudge. At that time, I didn't even realize what that experience taught me. The lessons we learn as children can affect us for the rest of our lives, if we aren't careful.

I'm pretty sure mom learned a lot from being abused, both physically and mentally, and needing to hide from my dad. She was such an emotionally unhealthy woman at that time. She couldn't make a decision for herself, let alone for my siblings and me. Frequently, I witnessed the abuse, and countless times I had to call the police, reporting my own father for domestic violence. I recall seeing my mom huddled up, wailing in grief and pain. It really hurt me to see my mother so devastated and broken.

"Forgiveness" and "becoming the change" are two themes I focus on when I speak to audiences. With kids, I share that we need to "become the change that we want to see in other people and in our lives." I talk about how I work every day to become a good person. I tell them that, "it is easy to be

> **"Without forgiveness, there is no future."**
> **- Desmond Tutu**

good to a person who is good to me; but to really be a good person, I am going to be good to those who aren't good to me." I have learned, in life we are constantly learning lessons, positive and negative. We must choose to be the change we want to see.

It wasn't always easy for me to forgive others who hurt me. Dealing with rejection from my parents and abuse from my father, I was hit hard by life's lessons. I remember at fourteen years old, I was looking for shelter with my brother and sister. We reached out to my grandmother, but she was elderly and scared of my dad. However, she was willing to take in my little sister Danielle. Unfortunately, she didn't have room for my baby brother or for me.

My best friend's aunt said, "Roy, I can take baby Ray, but I don't have room for you." Relieved that he would be alright, I told her, "Ms. Carmen, as long as I know he is safe and that he is eating, I will figure something out."

Not knowing where I would go, I went back to where we were staying, grabbed a bag, and packed it with items I thought I would need on the streets. I took neatly folded up clothes, my Bible, and a picture of my family. Fortunately, I tucked in a notepad and pen, which I used to keep a journal, just writing and writing what I was thinking and feeling. I started moving from home to home; living with whoever would take me in, for however long they would let me stay. I became what is known as a "couch surfer."

I tried to stay in school, but it was extremely difficult. I never knew where I would be living or if I would be able to make it to school. I would attend school one week and miss the entire next week, so eventually, I just stopped going.

At one point, I stayed with a family in Dallas, nearly 300 miles from my home in San Antonio, but it wasn't long before it was time for me to go. At this point in my life, this was a common thing. My heart had hardened a great deal, so it didn't affect me as much as it did when the first family asked me to leave. One family didn't even have the nerve to tell me it was time for me to go away. They dropped me off at a school event, telling me to call them when I was ready to be picked up. When I was done, I called and called. I wondered when they were coming, but after a while it dawned on me that they weren't. I always had my backpack with me, so I just moved on, again.

A family is all I wanted. The first family that took me in would say "Roy, mijo, we love you like a son," and I believed them. I would think… really? You love me? Maybe I found a home. When my birthday came along, they patted my shoulder and wished me a happy birthday. I was so excited that they remembered my birthday! Then, two weeks later, it was their real son's birthday, but he had a birthday party complete with candles and balloons. In my mind, I knew they didn't love me like a son. Now, maybe I should have been happy that I had a roof over my head and food in my mouth, but I was fourteen years old. I wanted to feel loved. I wanted a family.

Ultimately, I had to pack my bag once again, which left me wondering "What am I going to eat? Where am I going to sleep?" In 1997, I sneaked into an Omni Hotel in Dallas, hoping to find something to eat. They happened to be hosting the Federally Employed Women's conference at the time.

I crept into the conference and sat in the far right back corner just to get a free meal. Careful not to catch anyone's eye or seem out of place, I ate my food. A lady took the podium, but my only concern was eating. She caught my attention, though, when she spoke about her life and how she grew up. She was once told by her high school counselor that she would never accomplish anything in life. However, her father had taught her to ask, "Why not me?" This woman eventually became the highest ranking Latina woman in combat support for the U.S. Army.

As I sat there, I asked myself the same question. "Why not me? Why can't I have my dreams?" Why should I not succeed, just because I'm homeless and from a broken family? The only reason I didn't have my dreams was because I had stopped dreaming.

That day I decided I wasn't going to give up. I went back to San Antonio and got my baby brother back. I went to a minister of a church and said, "Pastor Doris, baby Ray and I, we have no place to live. But Ma'am if you let us live in your church, I promise you that we will clean it every Sunday and every Wednesday, and it will be ready for all your services." Pastor Doris, looked at me kindly, and said, "Roy, you're not going to live in my church. You're going to live with my husband and me."

She emphasized that we could live with them under one condition: I must return to high school. This was all that I wanted, to be "normal." I wanted to have a childhood. I wanted to make friends. So, I enrolled at Southwest High School as a third year freshman. I became a sophomore and then a senior. I was preparing for what would be the greatest moment of my life, high school graduation. I had never thought this day would come. I also never knew how much my education would change my life.

I went to community college and had a rocky start because I had lived in so many people' homes. When you couch surf, you learn to create a role. Every time I moved into a new house, I would look inside my imaginary bag and ask myself, "Who do these people want me to be?" I learned that if I could become the person they wanted me to be, I got to stay there a little longer. I could eat one more meal.

As a result, when I moved out on my own, I had taken on so many different personas that I had no clue who I was. Then one day, the Dean of the community college approached me, asking me to introduce a guest speaker. When I asked who the speaker was, I was shocked to find that she was retired Lieutenant Colonel Consuelo Castillo Kickbusch. This was the same woman who, seven years earlier at the Omni Hotel in Dallas, spoke those words that changed my life. Instantly, I agreed to introduce her. When I spoke to the audience, I told them that Lieutenant Colonel Kickbusch had given me a second chance at life with just her words, and that she never even knew it.

Two weeks later, I spoke at her book signing. Two weeks after that, her company hired me as an intern—a job that was supposed to last for three months but wound up lasting much longer. After two years, Lieutenant Colonel Kickbusch finally said, "Mijo, you know you have to go." At first, I thought I was being fired. But she explained that I needed to continue my education and finish college. She asked me where I wanted to go to school, but I didn't know because I would be the first in my family to graduate.

Following in Lieutenant Colonel Kickbusch's footsteps, I enrolled in Hardin-Simmons University in Abilene, Texas, and in 2009, I graduated with my degree in Business Marketing.

Three months before I graduated, my mentor, Lieutenant Colonel Kickbusch, called to ask if I would work for her company when I graduated. I told her that I was considering getting my Master's Degree in Pennsylvania, but she was persistent, asking me to make my decision before I got off the phone with her.

Confidently, I decided to work for her company. After graduation, I made the big move to Las Vegas, found a roommate, and unpacked everything I owned.

One morning Lieutenant Colonel Kickbusch called me to her office and said, "Roy, you have three months, and I am taking you off my payroll." In shock, all I could say was, "Excuse me?" She repeated herself, saying, "Look, mijo, if you work for me, you're never going to do what you're meant to do in life, and I'm not going to be responsible for that. You have three months to save up money and do whatever it is you think you need to do."

For the first month, I'm going to be honest—I was really upset with her. By the end of that month, I started wondering what I was going to do. One evening, before falling asleep on my roommate's couch, I said, "You know, God, I don't know what you want from me anymore. I don't know if you want me to keep speaking to students or if you want me to get a 9 to 5 job. I need you to guide me somewhere."

That night I had a dream. In the dream, I saw myself walking into an arena filled with young people who were clapping, cheering, and waving balloons. They weren't cheering for me, though. They were cheering because this conference was for young people who were fighting injustice throughout the world. I saw myself surrounded by

> *"Dreams are the touchstones of our character."*
> *-Henry David Thoreau*

them, and as a band played in the background, the young people sang, "Come on in, come on in, together we can make a difference. Come on in, come on in, together we can make a difference!" over and over again.

My roommate worked from nine at night until five in the morning. I woke up when he came in from work and frantically exclaimed, "Nick. Dude. I know what I need to do. I know what I *have* to do!" Nick, bewildered, had no idea what I was talking about. I simply replied, "I have to do a tour!" It was extremely early in the morning, and Nick watched me, confused, as I frantically packed my bag. I rushed out the door to the local Denny's®, and in a booth I started working on what became the "MyBag, MyHome, Homeless by Choice Tour."

Originally, I intended to travel from L.A. to Florida and speak at any school, organization, shelter, or company that was willing to open up their doors and share my message of perseverance, hope, and determination, and of the importance of a higher education. About mid-point of the tour, I started receiving so many letters, emails, and Facebook and MySpace messages from kids at schools I had visited sharing their heartbreaking stories with me. I had convinced myself that it wouldn't be hard to speak all over the nation, but I have to admit, it was probably the hardest task I have ever encountered.

Every presentation on the tour was pro bono, as long as the people were willing to open their doors. The reason it's called "Homeless by Choice" is because I chose to be homeless again, living the way I did as a teenager.

It's going to take all of us to make a difference. Every little bit helps. That's what the tour is all about. I intend to leave this country a little better by giving back, while I inspire the next generation to achieve.

Visit Roy Juarez's website www.homelessbychoice.org to learn more about the Homeless By Choice Tour and find out how you can help Roy's mission to advocate for those who are homeless, while teaching forgiveness.

Ordinary People™
Extraordinary Planet

Chapter 2

Russell K. Hayes

RUSSELL K. HAYES

They say that good things come in small packages. For Russell, his wife Carmen, and their six children, this proverb certainly rings true. Russell is the author of *Miracle Rugs based on a True Story*. This air ambulance pilot and former member of the United States Army helped to bring Matt Roloff from the critically-acclaimed TLC television series *Little People Big World* to help children who are dwarfs with disabilities in Iraq.

My youngest daughter was born via cesarean section at the regional hospital in Arecibo, Puerto Rico. I was not allowed in the operating room, nor did I really want to watch.

After the operation, the doctor came out and said, "You have a daughter, and she has short arms and short legs." I replied, "Of course she does. She was just born." Then he went on, "You don't understand me. Your daughter is a dwarf."

I asked if I could see her and went in the nursery, just minutes after she was born. When I saw her, I thought she was absolutely beautiful. I didn't quite understand. Then the doctor showed me that her arms and legs were disproportionate to the rest of her body.

Because she was born after visiting hours were over, I didn't get to stay at the hospital long. As soon as I got home, I jumped on the internet and typed in "dwarfism." While a lot of information popped up on my screen, what jumped out to me was an organization and support group called the Little People of America.

I called the organization the next day and spoke with a wonderful person named Monica Pratt. She explained dwarfism to me and how the Little People of America support group worked. We bought my daughter a lifetime membership that day.

I wanted to take an active role in encouraging my daughter to be a part of this support group. I realized that dwarfism was going to be a part of our lives and everything we do. She is going to have dwarfism for as long as she lives.

Let me rewind a bit, I used to be a helicopter pilot in the military. I was in the regular Army about 40 years ago and then off and on in the reserves.

In 2007, a few years after my daughter was born, I was in the reserve group called the "Individual Ready Reserve" or IRR. I wasn't an active reservist; I wasn't going to drills, nor was I part of the National Guard.

I would like to tell you a true story about a man named Abdul Salman from Baghdad, Iraq. He was working for the Americans and, along with his nephew, was helping build the new embassy there. As they were leaving a checkpoint from the

> *"If we cannot now end our differences, at least we can help make the world safe for diversity."*
> *- John Fitzgerald Kennedy*

Green Zone to the Red Zone (which is considered to be the more dangerous area) where they lived, they were approached by terrorists. "We know you're working for the infidels. We want you to help us kill a few of them." Abdul is an honorable man, and he and his nephew said "no." Not long after, he found a note tacked to his door that read, "Abdul and Ephrahim are marked for death." Abdul had three children who were handicapped dwarfs and two average-sized children. They managed to escape the country. Abdul warned his sister that she had to leave.

Abdul took his family to the Green Zone to hide in a shack. The next day, he found out through friends that his sister Naron and Ephrahim had been kidnapped. We later found out that his dear nephew died at 22 years old from complications due to being hung up and beaten by terrorists.

The Salman family had been through so much. Abdul's children who have dwarfism needed medical attention. Desperate, Abdul fell to his knees, praying for God to send angels to help his family. That same week or perhaps even the same day,

I was chosen from the list of Army aviators called back to active duty.

At the time, I wondered why in the world they were calling me up at my age. I never thought I'd be called back to active duty. It was my wife made me realize why. "Honey, why fight this? Maybe God has a reason for you to go to Iraq." I told her, "I can't fight the Army, you, and God."

The day my team arrived in Iraq, I emailed home to let everyone know I was safe and that it was hot as blazes there. Then, I checked the military's website to get the news of the day in Iraq. The first article that came up was about Abdul Salman, saying that he was helping the Americans. The last sentence jumped out at me: it said that three of his children had some type of dwarfism.

At that point, I heard my wife's words ringing in my ears, "Maybe God has a reason for you to go to Iraq."

Once I settled in, I asked my commander if I could visit Abdul's family. It was approved. When I met them, the children were mesmerized by the pictures of my daughter on my computer and stories about other dwarfs and the Little People of America conventions. It was the first time that they had seen dwarfs other than themselves, and they showed their appreciation for what I shared through lots of little hugs. Clearly they were happy to see me, and I truly fell in love with them.

The type of dwarfism these children have is Morquio Syndrome, and of all the types of dwarfism, it's the cruelest. What they eat, they can't metabolize. It puts deposits on their growth plates and bones, causing their bones to twist. Soon, it forms deposits on their organs. This type of dwarfism requires a lot of medical attention, which they unfortunately were unable to get.

When I found the Salman family in Iraq, I knew I needed to make connections with the media so we could get them help. I emailed all the talk shows. Then I recalled an important media connection. I had met Matt and Amy Roloff from the TV show *Little People Big World*, who have a son who also has dwarfism.

Matt and I were connected through the Little People of America organization from the time when I was an LPA Chapter President in Puerto Rico. I told him the story on the phone and said that I needed him to bring doctors and medical supplies. He asked me to email him pictures of the children and information, so they knew what they needed to bring. Matt came to Bagdad with a camera crew and the resources the Salman family desperately needed.

Abdul has become like a brother to me. As I mentioned, he is a very honorable man. He was paralyzed on the right side of his body when an Iranian mortar exploded next to him, wounding him in the head during the war. The left side of his face is still paralyzed, and he needs neurological surgery. He has gotten back partial use of his right side, though. He said that God truly answered his prayers when he met us.

I was unable to complete all that I had set out to do to help the Salman family during my first tour of duty, so I stayed behind for a second tour of duty when my unit went home. What took place during that second tour, as I helped the Salman family, was miraculous.

Because I was a member of the Individual Ready Reservists, I could be plugged into any unit that needed me. I was placed with the New Jersey National Guard for my second tour. When I met Colonel Schector, he looked at me a moment and then said, "I know you from someplace." He looked familiar to me too. He suggested that our military career paths must have crossed, but I had joined the Army forty years ago, when he was in grade school. Then during the conversation, I let him know that I had a daughter with dwarfism. His jaw dropped. "I have a son with dwarfism." Then we shared pictures of our children. It turns out, we'd both been to every LPA convention for the past 11 years. Most likely, we had walked right past each other at the conventions. The conventions have thousands of people, so we had never been introduced.

It seems to me that God activated two parents of dwarves to be in Baghdad a mile away from where the Salman family was hiding. While helping them, we both had our own children in the back of our minds.

14

The results of the second tour made it possible for my wife and I to sponsor them. We brought the whole family plus the interpreters to America: a total of 14 Iraqis. I filled out the State Department paperwork, stating that I would sponsor the family and make sure that they are able to integrate into society. They now live in Kuna, Idaho, right next door to our house.

Saja was the oldest of their three children with dwarfism and our inspiration to do all that we did. When I first stepped foot in her house in Iraq, she was so happy to meet me, thrilled to learn that other dwarfs existed besides her siblings. I laid some gifts near her, and sweet Saja kissed them. The interpreter told me that she loved what I brought her. Saja said with a playful smile, "How about a kiss?" My heart melted. As I held her incredibly tiny body, I felt her warmth and love. I knew I had to help in any way that I could.

The progression of her Morquio Syndrome had left her unable to walk. When we brought her to the states, we were anxious for her to have an important operation so she could retain the small bit of mobility she had. She was only able to roll around on the floor.

We needed to straighten her spine and fuse her neck so she could sit up and use a wheelchair. It was her first time in a hospital.

During the surgery, her heart actually stopped beating two times and one of her lungs collapsed. Unfortunately, dear Saja did not survive the surgery and passed away, dying in my arms in the ICU. When we knew that she was going, I held onto her until her spirit left her body. It was like losing one of my own children. It was very difficult. Abdul and I cried in each other's arms.

When you sponsor a family, you assume some financial responsibility. I was retired, so my wife and I spent our savings and our retirement — everything we had was spent on Saja. After that surgery, my wife and I were tapped out. Now we are starting a foundation to raise money for the life-saving operations that the last two children need.

A doctor in Delaware, who is very familiar with Morquio syndrome, is willing to take them on as patients, but we need funding to get them there for three to six months. We're hoping and praying for a miracle at this time.

My wife Carmen and I started the International Dwarf Advocacy Association (IDAA) to help people with dwarfism and their families all over the world. Our foundation helps with their medical and financial needs. Our goal is to help them be successful and adapt to their local environments or help them relocate if needed.

Abdul once called me his "angel." I flew in on metal wings and did everything I could to make their lives better. For whom or for what cause will you be an angel? I want to encourage you to find your calling and help someone who can't help themselves today. No matter how little a difference you think you can make, one simple act can make a world of difference to someone in need.

You can visit www.dwarfchildren.org to help Russell in his personal mission to get Ali and Baraa Salman the life-saving medical care they need.

Ordinary People™
Extraordinary Planet

Chapter 3

Arturo Sandoval

Photo Credit: Manny Iriarte

ARTURO SANDOVAL

Trumpeter and composer Arturo Sandoval possesses "some of jazz's fiercest chops," according to *The New York Post*, and has been recognized with many remarkable honors. Arturo won four Grammy Awards, six Billboard Awards, and two Emmys. He was given the Key to Miami, recorded over ten albums, and performed for a President of the United States. Arturo plays alongside stars such as Celine Deion, Alicia Keys, Harry Connick, Jr., and Charlotte Church. He is a Professor at Florida International University in Miami, allowing him the distinguished honor of shaping minds and passing on his love of music. Also, Arturo inspired HBO to make a movie about his life, *For Love or Country: The Arturo Sandoval Story*, which documented how he escaped from Castro's Communist rule over Cuba to go on to be one of the world's greatest horn players of all time.

You know, yesterday was a long day. Unbelievable. In the morning, when I got to the LAX airport, they said my flight was cancelled. I said, "Oh my goodness, don't tell me that. I have a concert tonight in Washington, D.C.!" The airline people started working on a plan and finally put me on a plane to Dallas, Texas, and then on another plane. I got to the club at exactly 8 o'clock. I didn't even stop in the hotel or warm up or anything. I went from the airport straight to the stage. But it was beautiful last night . . . great audience, great people – people who actually waited for me to arrive. People who really enjoyed the music. We had a lot of fun.

Some trips can be a bit eventful and others can be life-changing.

Mine is the life of a musician. I have been playing on the music scene "only" 50 years. I was born in Cuba in 1949. I would say the music saved my life. I say this because I was so poor, my family was so poor. We were starving there. Oh my goodness, you won't believe how poor we were. In my house, we didn't even have floors. They were dirt.

I was probably 9 or10 years old when I really started in music. It was at that age that I knew I had a dream in my heart, a passion for music, and that it was going to be my way out. When I first verged on this passion, I was living in a village in the middle of nowhere. I joined up with some kids in a village nearby. They put together a marching band and they gave us several instruments to try. I wasn't even sure what I liked until the day I heard the trumpet. Its bold, hearty sound was like warm, smooth honey – sweet, rich, and golden – pouring over my soul. I felt enveloped by its call, and I knew that was the instrument for me.

I went to the teacher and told him my decision, but he said they didn't have any trumpets left. "What about if I find a trumpet? Will you let me play in the band?" When he said that he would, my aunt bought me a pocket cornet.

Armed with my horn, I went to an old man in my village who had a reputation as a good trumpet player and trumpet teacher. "Can you teach me how to play this?" He told me to play something for him. "I don't know how to play any songs," I said, so I blew into the cornet, and some sounds came out. He was a cranky old man, and after a few seconds he said, "You know what? Put that chunk of metal back in the case, and I'm going to give you some advice. Don't waste your time and my time, because you have no talent at all for that. I recommend that you try another instrument." Of course, after hearing that, I sobbed all the way home.

When I got there, I wiped away my tears and said, "You know what? This guy is not God. He's wrong." I sat down with my cornet under a mango tree and blew that thing until blood came out of my mouth. It became my hobby, my ambition, my escape. Unfortunately, that grumpy old man passed away soon after, so I never had a chance to play something for him. But the only lesson I ever had from him was invaluable, because if I am told I can't do something, I do it. I go for it.

In my family, nobody has anything to do with art, nobody. My father was a great mechanic. Then, the Revolution took away his ability to have his own garage. But, while I didn't come from a family of musicians, music came to save me.

Man, when I heard my first Dizzy Gillespie and Charlie Parker records, I couldn't believe it. I said, "Wow! Goodness, what kind of music is that?" I was in love with it. I heard the album over twenty years after it was recorded because we weren't allowed to listen to jazz or "the music of the Imperialists," as the government called it. In fact, Cuba didn't have any record stores at all at that time. But I couldn't resist the music. And listening to Dizzy play that horn made me practice even harder.

Even though it was forbidden, I would listen to a short-wave radio show, Willis Conover's Jazz Hour on the Voice of America. During my obligatory military service, at 21 years of age, I was caught listening to "the radio of the enemies" and was thrown in jail. I was locked up for three and a half months without my horn. My parents could only visit me for a few minutes every two weeks.

> *"Music produces a kind of pleasure which human nature cannot do without."*
> *- Confucius*

In Cuba, you have to lie if you love freedom. You have to be like an actor to survive. When I would go on stage around the world, I had to thank "la Revolución." To protect my family, I found ways to get around the oppression. Like, when the band realized that we needed to perform jazz, we came up with a new sound but with a familiar feel. To cover up the jazz, the congas were placed in front, and my band Irakere began playing the new Cuban music. We had Paquito D'Rivera on sax and Chucho Valdes on the piano. The people of Cuba loved Irakere.

One great day, I found out that my hero Dizzy Gillespie was coming to Cuba. I went to the port where he would arrive. When he got off the boat, he wanted to see a Cuban musician whom I knew. The government people who were sent to pick him up couldn't help, so I jumped in and said that I could drive him to meet the performer. I showed him my island. We listened to local musicians play guaguanco and rumba in the streets. The government people took him to see my band, Irakere. When he saw me wailing on my instrument, Dizzy laughed. "What the hell is my driver doing with a trumpet?" Dizzy and I became great friends, and I learned so much from him. He even called me his "Cuban son."

In 1981, my own country nominated and gave me the award for Best Musician of Cuba. Everybody from around the island got to vote in a magazine, so it was a competition where the people chose the winner. They gave me that award nine times before I left. From '82 through '90 I was considered Cuba's Best Instrumentalist. Of course, I was getting all this recognition while I was in Cuba, playing the music that I was passionate about playing.

I also won the 1978 and 1990 Grammies for Best Latin Album. Now don't get confused – at the time I won those Grammies, we were living in Cuba. But the Grammy was over in America, you know, so we couldn't accept it in person. I was in my "home country." Of course, Cuba was my country, but the government was really holding me back. They let me play only to show off my skills when it benefitted them.

I knew that I had to get out of Cuba. When I fell in love with my wife Marianela and found out that she worked for the government, it got more complicated. As time passed, it became trickier to leave. She had a son when we met, and then we had a baby, and for a long time she believed in Castro's Revolution.

Being unable to leave by your own free will, having to escape from *your own country* makes you feel like you killed someone or you did something horrible. It's hard. The experience was scary.

The embassy started off saying that because I was able to play music, I wasn't being persecuted. They said I was only doing it so I could make more money. It's not about the money, though; it was about the music. When you know that someone might come to your house and hurt you because of a song . . . that *is* persecution.

It's difficult to describe how it feels to escape from your own country, your home. You have this torn apart, empty feeling leaving your country that way. But finally, we did it.

While I was touring in Europe in 1990, my family was given a special pass by the Cuban government to join me in London, which was an exceptional moment. That was the opportunity I was looking for. Usually the government doesn't allow the families to leave the island. It was a rare and special exception to do such a thing. Once I had my family in Europe with me, I took my chance.

> *"Life is something like a trumpet. If you don't put anything in, you won't get anything out."*
> *- William Christopher Handy*

At the time, I was playing horn with Dizzy for the United Nations Band, and he knew what I was going through. Dizzy took me to the American Embassy in Rome, and they opened the doors for us that night. I told them that I had to flee Cuba, my own country, for freedom and asked for political asylum. After all the questioning and Dizzy calling the Vice President of the United States to explain, I was reunited with my Marianela and my youngest son, and we were able to live in Miami together.

Family is important to me. My parents finally escaped Cuba in a raft three years later and were rescued off the shores of Florida. My older son and his wife eventually joined us.

Yes, the United States is my country. You know, I was born and raised in Cuba, but I love the U.S. and appreciate so much what this country has done for me and my family and what it means for us. I'm so pleased. I got my citizenship in 1999, and I'm happy and proud to be an American.

I want to spend the rest of my life here. Anywhere you go where the people respect and admire what you do and embrace you and your career – that's your place. That's your home. It doesn't matter if you weren't born there. People can completely integrate into this country, including everything it stands for. I *am* completely integrated into the United States.

I speak more than one language, but music is absolutely a language of its own. It's the only one everybody understands around the world. Music is universal.

Many call me "The Latin Jazz Trumpeter," but I feel uncomfortable with that title because I am a musician of all kinds of music. I started out playing classical trumpet at the Cuban National School of the Arts, and now, several of my recordings are of classical music. I love music, period. All of it. I try to embrace the music without any discrimination, regardless of style. That's my goal, and that's my thing.

As I told the *Orlando Sentential*, "Music was my salvation, a piece of wood floating in the ocean. I told myself, 'OK, grab this and you'll be able to save yourself and help your family.'" Now, I have two granddaughters from my two sons. My wife and I have had a beautiful relationship and friendship for almost 37 years of marriage. Because of the music, my family and I have a great life together in America.

Arturo performs many concerts for St. Jude's Children's Research Hospital. In fact, they named him their Man of the Year. To find out more about how you can contribute to St. Jude's, please visit www.stjude.org.

Chapter 4

Xiaobo LaPresta
黄小波

XIAOBO LAPRESTA

Xiaobo Huang LaPresta came from Shanghai and found amazing love in the United States, when she married Jack, an Italian-American. During their 22 years together, they lived the American dream, beginning with a small bakery and eventually working with Berk Enterprises, a thriving importing and exporting business. Her story will be featured in a documentary created by Dream Catchers Films, Inc., hosted by Dr. Shellie Hipsky called *Xiaobo and Jack's Recipe for Love*. Xiaobo's cross-cultural tale is one of happiness, loss, and healing as she copes with the death of her true love and moves forward with her life.

My Dear and Wonderful Xiaobo,

You are the most beautiful and most charming wife in the whole world. You are the best, and everything that a husband could want. We have so much to be thankful for; we share a wonderful life together. When I think about our journey in life, all that we went through, and where we are now, it makes me want to cry and then laugh. I love you more than all the rice in China, my love for you is like a river bubbling over. Thanks for the good memories, and thanks for the wonderful journey we have had together in life.

Love,

Jack

- From a Card written on the LaPresta's 20th Wedding Anniversary

One day in 1985, in the middle of packing to leave campus after graduating from East China Normal University in Shanghai (上海华东师范大学), I met a young Jewish lawyer, Paula Kasler, in the university's library. We began chatting, and she asked if she could visit with my mother – an author and lawyer – to learn about Chinese law. Over the next few weeks, we travelled together in China and became close friends. Then, Paula offered to sponsor my move to the United States by paying my living expenses there. So, with only 60 dollars in my pocket, I came to the United States to get my master's degree in education. To this day, Paula is like a sister to me.

For the first six months, I lived with Paula in San Francisco. Then, in August, I received a scholarship and moved to Ohio to attend the University of Akron. In January, a schoolmate introduced me to his friend Jack.

His smile was penetrating and contagious; he smiled from his heart with those shining eyes. We dated and fell in love. Before marriage, I never asked him how much money he had. I told Jack, "America is the land of opportunity, and we both are hard-working people. We will be successful." Because we had unconditional love from the beginning, we knew our marriage would be strong, even with few material things. I still cherish my $99 wedding ring and my beautiful Italian lace wedding dress, found in a Salvation Army Store, as much as any princess would value the symbols of her own wedding day. We were not able to afford the air tickets to invite any of my Chinese family, but they were there in spirit.

At our wedding, I giggled when my Jack lifted me high in his arms and said into the video camera, "I want to thank your parents for having such a beautiful daughter like Xiaobo to come into my life and bring me such happiness. I am so glad that your daughter is as light as a feather; I could carry her all over the United States!"

Soon, I started helping Jack in his little bakery a couple of steps away from our house. My life quickly changed from my old Chinese ways to pizza, pepperoni rolls, and neighborhood kids playing pinball games. In our Italian pizza shop, I sold Chinese fans and silks. Two years later, I added on a Chinese restaurant in front of the bakery.

Wearing his silly red, white, and green chef's hat, Jack would throw the dough high in the air to make the hot pepper and cheese bubble bread for our customers. His over 70-year-old father and mother spread the marinara sauce on the pizza shells beside him. Jack and I would sing fun songs as we baked the food, filled with spicy pepperoni and love. In the bakery, we worked 24/7 together.

We didn't make much money, but we were so connected to each other. Our Christmas gifts during the hard times were not store-bought. Instead, we would write precious notes to each other. I treasured these more than any expensive gift.

Because we had very little parking space, after a while, we decided to sacrifice our house to extend the parking lot. It was painful to see the big bulldozer demolish our house. We had to live in the bakery with some of our employees from China.

We laughed as we slept with hats on, because the bakery was very cold. One time, we sat overnight, hand-in-hand, waiting for the pizza shell dough to rise, so we could deliver them to the Canfield Fair the next morning. From memories such as these, I learned that communication, commitment, and being supportive of each other are important in a marriage.

We shared the basic vision for our business, which was, of course, to make more money, but we decided to take a risk and change our career direction. Jack supported me in all the types of jobs I tried over the years, including selling makeup door-to-door, selling health insurance, being a financial advisor, and opening a clothing boutique. I knew that, in order to fulfill our dreams, we needed to use our heads, instead of just working the dough and frying eggrolls forever.

Early on, we discovered that home is wherever you have love. Jack and I were blessed with an adorable daughter Mae, who made our family complete. With our dog Pikachu, we started our journey toward the American dream.

I opened a learning center in which I taught everything from Tai Chi to the Chinese language. Jack used to joke that the big sign in the storefront window that listed all the classes I offered read like a book because I was doing so much.

It was hard to make ends meet, even here in this land that I once thought would be paved with gold. Jack transported people to the airport and hospital for money. I sold everything we had, including our Persian cat and his father's wine press. We had to pay the bills.

Although we needed money, Jack knew that I needed to stay connected to my culture. He supported me as I volunteered as president of the Chinese Association of Greater Youngstown. Jack and I invited my mother, Ou Yangcui (欧阳翠), and my father, Huangbinlin (黄彬琳), a graduate from Huang Pu Military Academy, to stay with us in 1989, when I became a U.S. citizen. Jack grew very close to them and took good care of my father when he was sick. They did not want to leave after visiting us for a year.

When I was a child, I would often cry in the bathroom by myself, while my parents fought over money. I didn't want that for my life. I wanted to have a happy husband and a family. They were both nice people, just not a good match. They did not plan together in financial matters. An old Chinese saying states that "If a couple separates money, their hearts are separated as well." For 31 years, I was worried about their marriage. With Jack's help, I realized that I no longer had to carry their marital pain as my burden. I was able to put that worry aside and focus on my own marriage.

Our marriage was so much fun! We loved to spoil each other. We considered it a privilege to sacrifice and compromise for each other. Couples should always try to be romantic and make each other laugh. Do more than just asking routinely, "How are you today?" A hug or kiss with real feelings, a surprise note in the lunchbox, a funny voicemail, a flower brought in from the garden – these shouldn't be saved for a special day. Showing affection is part of a healthy, strong marriage.

What I really miss is the fun. Jack and I made each other laugh every day. We treated each other like king and queen, and we called our little "Snow White cottage" a castle. Our relationship got better as our marriage continued. Jack whispered in my ear often, "I thought I got silver, but you are gold, I am the richest man in the world. The only thing I regret is not meeting you earlier. God threw away the mold after making Xiaobo."

A loyal soul mate will make you feel so safe and special. Bring the best out in each other. Don't compete with each other. Know his potential. Be patient. Sometimes things aren't going to go as planned. Let him fall down in life, let him get back up by himself, and then draw conclusions about handling the situation to avoid making the same mistakes. With respect, we agreed to never embarrass each other in public. Problems were always discussed privately, and we had family meetings often at the dinner table.

Our marriage was a sweet one. The business was not easy to maintain, but we didn't fail. Rather, we chose another direction. I convinced him to become a salesman, because he was so people-oriented, and he was great at it. We were finally making the money.

As for me, I was teaching Chinese at Youngstown State University, when I found out that Berk Enterprises needed a translator for the importing/exporting food packaging business. Soon, I moved into the role of importing manager. Jack and I made a big commitment to help Mr Berk, because he told us the importing business was new for him. We weren't working together anymore, and I had to go into the office every day, frequently working nights, due to the time difference in China. Fortunately, our foundation was very strong. We couldn't wait to see each other at night.

During the first four years, Jack and I helped Berk's business to expand rapidly. I got lots of good advice from Jack. When I started working for the company we would only ship four 40-foot-long shipping containers (each would fill the back of a semi-truck) monthly. Now we ship 50 to 90 of these huge containers every month!

Almost every year, Jack, Mr. Berk, and I visited the Chinese factory (our supplier) and were greeted with fireworks and even a colorful Chinese dragon dance. On a stage, the 300 factory workers sang and danced to express their thanks for helping them to export what they made. We felt so appreciated for our hard work that it brought tears to our eyes. "You are pretty sharp in business," my boss, Mr. Rob Berk, said. Jack would be so happy to see I have been working for Berk's for over 11 years, and Berk is continuing to do well globally under the good leadership of Mr. Berk and Frank Valley.

We were raising our beautiful daughter to learn the best of both cultures and to believe in serving and helping others. Mae wrote to us for our 20th wedding, "You are a model couple. You hardly ever fight, and you love each other more than anyone I know. I know that as far as parents go, you are as good as it gets." She went on to be valedictorian in Canfield High School and is now studying at The Ohio State University.

Then, after Jack and I had been married 22 years, during exploratory surgery, everything went horribly wrong. The doctor came out to me and said that Jack's fingers had turned black, and they had to cut them off of his hand. I told them, "Just give me back my husband." Then the doctor said that his toes were black, and I screamed, "Take them off, just bring me my Jack!" After this happened to one of his limbs, I was crying so hard. I just wanted my husband. I didn't care if he couldn't walk, I just needed my Jack. Unfortunately, he passed away.

When he died, I thought my life was completely over. My heart was broken when we buried him. I read the following speech at his funeral in front of over a thousand people:

1-9-2009

Hi, Jack,

Just want to let you know that you are my hero. I am so proud of you for all the things you accomplished. I want to thank you for making me the happiest person in the world for the last 22 years and helping me fulfill the American dream. I was extremely fortunate to have a best friend and soul mate like you.

I want to thank the person who invented "marriage," because being married was the best time of my life. I learned so much from you. We had a unique bond, always knowing the thoughts on one another's minds. Luckily we did not waste a minute of our time together. Every day, we could not wait to come home to see each other; we always had so much to talk and laugh about. We did not care where we were or what we were doing, as long as we were together, like "sticky rice." Our love was so deep and selfless, we would die for each other.

I also want to tell you that you should be so proud of your beautiful family. During this heartbreaking time, I was greatly touched by the deep love, caring, and support I received from our daughter, your sisters, your brothers-in-law, your nieces, your nephews, your school friends, your friends from everywhere, your neighbors, and our Highway Tabernacle church friends. They were with me day and night; I cannot imagine what would have happened to me without their support. I know you want me to thank all of them today.

I know you always wanted my sister from China to visit, to show her how we lived. Xiaolin is here in the United States for the first time today, along with Jerry Yu (余建麟) from New York, who is the president of United Pacific, and your German shepherd dog club colleagues. Paula, my friend who brought me to this country, is also here from California. Your brother-in-law, Ralph Detoro, your good friend Pat Pilolli, and even your favorite boxer, Aunt Stella's grandson, Kelly Pavlik, the Lightweight World Champion are here, as well. Dr. Pek Chiew Teh (郑百洲陈芝华医师夫妇) and Pat Pilolli, will talk shortly.

You left me beautiful memories that will stay with me forever. People told us we had a fairytale love, which was so powerful that it obliterated all the obstacles, and any age gap, and cultural barriers. I know you want me to be strong and happy. I will treasure these memories and won't let you be disappointed.

Today I want to celebrate your life. You lived the best life, and you deserved the best. You had no regrets. And today I am not going to say good-bye, because you did not go anywhere. I will hold your hand and never let go. You are in my blood, and you are in my heart forever. May peace be with us always.
Love,
Xiaobo

31

After the funeral, I was beyond exhaustion. I felt like I was barely able to breathe. Jack took all my joy with him, and I felt like I was dying. I was not able to face the reality: my dream, our ideal home, built over 22 years was destroyed in two weeks. My girlfriend, Sheng Chunmei (盛春妹, 董事长, 中国顶华进出口公司) flew in from China, just to take care of me. She called my sister and told her I was a changed and broken woman. My sister heard me on the phone and said that I could not die in America. I needed to come home. "If she needs to be carried to Shanghai, she must be here with us!" Soon after the funeral, my daughter left for college, and I found myself alone. It was hard to face the reality.

For more than a year, my sisters, Du Mengpu (杜梦璞), Huang Yunyun (黄运运), and Huang Xiaolin (黄小琳); my brother, Du Xiangang (杜□刚); and many special girlfriends took care of me 24 hours a day, accompanied me to doctor appointments, and slept by my side.

"Xiaobo Remember what is to be remembered; forget what is to be forgotten."
- Huang Zong Ying (黄宗英), Chinese writer and actress

Back in Shanghai, my family couldn't understand why I was so pained. They said I was "greedy" because I had 22 years with my soul mate, and some people never have one. Traditionally, Chinese people are given 49 days to grieve and then move on after the death of a family member. After they read our love letters, they realized how big my loss was. Some famous Chinese authors who are friends of the family wrote about my story, which will be published in my upcoming book. My mother said, "You fell down from heaven into hell."

I thought I would never love again. My family wanted me to find a nice Chinese man to take care of me into my old age, but my heart was in America. I missed my daughter and our dog terribly. Also, my sweet sisters-in-law: Joann King, Gigi

Gianinni, and Terri Detoro who have treated me as their real sisters were on my mind. The United States had been my home for over 22 years. I told my family I received so much love in there and needed to go back to thank everyone.

I admire husbands and wives who grow old together, and although I was unable to do this with Jack, I longed for someone who I could grow old with. My friend Rose Chait, helped me to post my profile on Match.com and screen the men. It was a big step for me, and I was little scared. I never imagined dating in my fifties. Eventually, I began talking to a man named Jay Liebowitz on Match, though, and I soon started looking forward to his messages.

After we chatted on the phone for 7 weeks, I made a date with Jay, a business professor and Jewish-American from Pittsburgh. We met at the mall. My two friends, my sister, and I checked Jay out as he sat in the food court clutching roses and chocolates for me. Less than a week later, Jay and I had Thanksgiving dinner at Jack's sister's house with thirty Italian relatives. They were very welcoming to Jay because they love me, and they encouraged me to date him, knowing Jack would want me to be happy.

Jay is very open-minded about everything. It is new for him to date a widow, and he's very supportive and patient. At first, I was a little scared. Then when I opened up, Jay took it well. Jack became a positive influence on our relationship. Jay says, "Jack is watching over us, and I would imagine he's pretty happy that Xiaobo has found another nice guy. I know how much they loved each other." I have been seeing Jay for six months now. I am thankful Jay is a thoughtful, smart, hardworking, and loving person.

After Jack passed away, I delayed the real grieving process. I refused to say goodbye to Jack in my heart for a long time, because I was confused by some of the advice I received. Thinking I could distract myself, I traveled to places like Hawaii, Japan, and New York. Everywhere I went made me sad, because I wished Jack was sharing those beautiful scenes with me. Finally, I went to the Good Grief Center in Pittsburgh.

They analyzed my case and explained that I had not only suffered the sudden loss of my husband, but also my soul mate, business partner, and "baby" – when Mae left for college – all at the same time. Jack was so much to me. While it was good to hear others' stories, I still struggled with his being gone. Yet, through the tears, I made it my goal to recover and help others like me.

Telling our story for the documentary and books like this one are part of my personal healing process. Lots of people encouraged me to tell my stories, especially after I made two wedding speeches at my niece's and nephew's weddings to over 700 hundred people in Shanghai. In fact, many people call and email me for love advice. Jack and I introduced seven couples, who are all still married. They call me "the loving family expert."

When people read my beautiful story in a magazine, they are amazed, because most people think that type of love is only found in fairytales.

I will continue to honor Jack LaPresta's memory so my future grandchildren will know what a loving and special man Jack was.

In an extraordinary journey worthy of an ancient Chinese fable, love led me through laughter and tears, from pizza to silk, from my native country to America, back to the land of my birth, and finally to my home.

Xiaobo recommends giving to the One Foundation, which is led by action movie star Jet Li; Jackie Chan was formerly the honorary director-general. This Red Cross Society foundation's four pillars of focus are education, health, environment, and poverty in China. Go to www.onefoundation.cn to see how you can help through volunteering or philanthropy.

Xiaobo acknowledges a few of the many people who helped her during her dark times:

Wang Anyi (王安忆, 中国作家协会副主席), the vice president of the Chinese Writers' Association; Wang Xiuwen (王修文，新东方教科集团总裁兼北京新东方扬州外国语学校校长副), the vice president of the New Oriental Education & Technology Group, China; Shanghai Television Station (上海电视台外语频道); E. Gordon Gee, president of The Ohio State University; Lin Xu (许林), director of the Chinese School Association in the United States (全美中文学校协会常务理事); Pu Ying (浦瑛, 伊利华报社长), the president of the Erie Chinese Journal; Mr. Frank Rulli, the president of Rulli Brothers Super Markets, Youngstown, Ohio; Zhou Tian (周天，金鸡奖最佳科教片奖得主), my brother-in-law, a writer and the 1982 winner of the China Golden Rooster Award; Jiang JinCheng (姜金城中国作家协会会员), writer; Peng XinqQi (彭新琪, 中国作家协会会员), writer; Cao Gang (曹钢, 上海星洲文化传媒有限公司执行董事), executive director of Shanghai Xingzhou Culture Media Co.; Zhou Qing (周晴，上海少年儿童出版社副总编辑), my niece and the deputy cditor of Shanghai Children's Publishing House; Huazan (华赞), president of Future Trends International Group Corporation; Brian Linden (林登), executive director of Linden Center (喜林苑); Dr.Yee Chung and Diane Ho (何宜中医师夫妇); Dr. Kong and Gim Oh; Dr. Tec Lee; Dr. Zhifeng Huo (霍志峰), chairman of U.S. Shandong Fellowship Association Education Funds (美国山东同乡会教育基金主席); Tai Chi Qigong Master Lin Housheng (林厚省，国际气功联合总会主席); Huang Qiong (黄琼), executive officer of Accura Tax & Accounting, LLC, (达捷税收会计事务所总裁); Xu Chang (许畅，上海油画家), my nephew and Shanghai oil painter.

Chapter 5

Bryan Mark Rigg

BRYAN MARK RIGG

Bryan Mark Rigg's impressive contributions to the study of history have been noted in *The New York Times*, on Fox News, and on NBC Dateline. The Federal German Military Archives in Germany house the "Bryan Mark Rigg Collection" with documents, visuals, and memoirs that this acclaimed author/historian acquired. He graduated with honors from highly respected universities. Bryan served as an officer in the U.S. Marine Corps and he has his own firm called "Rigg Wealth Management." However, he was once thought to be "brain damaged."

Soon after I was born, my mom noticed that I was always struggling with things that other babies didn't. For instance, I had a hard time going to sleep. Then, at about 6 or 7 months old, I started bouncing my head off my crib, and as I got older, I would do it on my pillow. Now, we know that some children who are hyperactive do this. It's called "crib-rocking." It's basically done to stimulate the mind.

Many times, people who are hyperactive have a difficult time sitting still and paying attention in school. It is because they are not getting enough stimulation to maintain focus. That is why it is so imperative for hyperactive children to have a healthy dose of athletic activity daily. I think it is so crazy that, here in America, many public schools have actually stopped offering recess.

At school, during Pre-K, kindergarten, and so on, I had a difficult time with the teachers and struggled with sitting still. My mother wanted to know why.

After I failed first grade for the second time, my mom took me to the Child Study Center and was shocked by what they told her. My diagnosis was "MBD," which is what it was called back then. Horrifyingly, the acronym stands for "minimal brain damage." This term has been upgraded to "ADHD" or "attention-deficit hyperactivity disorder," today. I also have dyslexia and had a speech impediment.

The doctor told her that I, most likely, would not graduate high school. He gave her some reports to read, which said that people with my profile frequently resort to criminal activity. She was given scientific data on this.

Depending on the studies you look at, anywhere between 8 to 12% of the population today are labeled with ADHD and 70 to 80% of inmates have ADHD.

Many first graders are excited to go to school, but I wasn't. I was held back and then held back again, while all of my friends were moving on without me to higher grades. It was a difficult time because the church that my family went to, Pantego Bible Church, housed Pantego Christian Academy where I went to school. I had to see the same friends at church, but they were in different grades from me. I stayed a first grader for three years.

Kids can be brutal to one another in every culture, and America is no different. I felt like I had a big bull's-eye on my forehead because of my learning problems.

My speech impediment made it difficult to pronounce words well. Obviously, when I was held back, the kids were rough on me. The playground would ring with "Moron Rigg," "Freak Rigg," and "Alien Rigg." I was teased daily because I was different.

My self-esteem was extremely low from all the teasing, and if you don't have self-esteem, you won't learn at all.

By this time, my mom was having nightmares of her 20-year-old son driving to his own sixth grade graduation. She knew she needed to do something drastic. Luckily, my mom got a piece of advice from the Child Study Center that actually helped.

Dr. Stephen Maddox, who had diagnosed me, suggested Texas Christian University, which has a special lab school. Lab schools are connected to a university, and this one focused on kids with severe learning disabilities.

My mom talked to Laura Lee Crane, who was head of the Starpoint School at Texas Christian University (TCU) at the time, to see if they would accept me.

The Starpoint School was formed especially for children like me. The Neely family in Fort Worth, Texas, was a very prominent, wealthy family. They had a grandson with such extreme learning issues that no school wanted to take him. The family set up their lab school at TCU and invited some well-known teachers from New York City to teach.

By the time I got there, I hated school. I couldn't read, write, or do simple math. I always sat in the back of the room, and out of sheer frustration, I would break my pencils and rip my homework up because I just couldn't do it.

> *"Every one of us is different in some way, but for those of us who are more different, we have to put more effort into convincing the less different that we can do the same thing they can, just differently."*
> *- Marlee Matlin*

My first week there, I sat down with a wonderful teacher, Mary Stewart. When she heard about all my struggles, she gave me a big hug. Of course, this was when teachers were still allowed to hug their students. She said, "Bryan, you're not a freak and you're not abnormal. You're not 'learning disabled.' You are 'learning different.' I'm here to help you find your strengths."

The school had no grades like "As" or "Bs". You worked at your own pace. The rewards were special events, so if you did well in behavior, reading, or math you would earn little chips. When you had a certain amount of chips, you would be able to go to TCU's swimming pool at the end of the week, to the Olympic pool and jump off the high dive, to the football stadium where TCU played football, to the zoo, and so on. If you didn't do well, then your privileges were taken away.

Finally, I started to thrive in this environment. By the end of the first year, I went from being an eight-year-old who couldn't read at all to reading books at the junior-high level and doing geometry and algebra.

I fondly recall a conversation with a teacher who said, "Bryan, remember all of those kids who called you 'freak'" and 'abnormal'? You are now reading books at a higher level than they are! What does that tell you about their commentary? It tells you they didn't know what you were capable of accomplishing. Remember, when people criticize and label you, they're telling you more about themselves than about you."

Most adults know instinctively that when people criticize others, they are showing their own wounded souls. However, many of us still react emotionally to this, especially as children.

Mary's words on my first day at Starpoint got me over that emotional hump. My wife, Stephanie, says Mary gave me a "bullet-proof self-esteem." If somebody is criticizing me, it's very easy for me to ignore it. On the other hand, if somebody provides constructive criticism, I am eager to embrace it. That was one of her greatest lessons. She healed my self-esteem and gave me the tools to learn.

When I would act up in class at Starpoint, I was always redirected to something productive. Mary wouldn't make me feel like I was in trouble. At my previous schools, I was paddled — it was the mid 1970s — for my "bad behavior." Every whack would add a sense of shame. Instead of inflicting pain, Mary made me think about my responsibility for my actions by saying things like, "Bryan, do you think that is a wise choice?"

At one point, my mom felt forced to put me on Ritalin medication. She had me try it for a while, but she thought I looked like I was suffering from rickets. It took away my personality, and I lost my appetite. My condition upset her.

A report Dr. Maddox gave her explained that people who think they need to have drugs to behave normally will rely on the pill instead of themselves for proper behavior. Medication takes away their ability to control their own behavior. The report horrified my mom, so she started doing some more research.

An all-natural diet had been developed by a doctor, Benjamin Feingold, who believed that the more natural your child's diet is, the better off your child's health and behavior is going to be. A lot of anecdotal evidence showed that when hyperactive kids went on all-natural diets, they started to behave "normally" and were able to study.

My brilliant mom got everybody on-board with the idea: my coaches, teachers, and friends' parents were encouraging me to eat an all-natural diet. I couldn't eat artificial flavors, artificial colors, or preservatives. She read all the ingredients on everything she fed me. That diet transformed my life.

The Child Study Center in Fort Worth also documented that, when my mom shifted me to an all-natural diet, my behavior improved. Following football games, the rest of the kids had Cokes, but my mom always made sure I had juice. After school when most kids had cookies and Kool-Aid, my mom had orange juice and a banana ready. She was on top of it.

With my diet changed around, armed with a better elementary school experience, and my self-esteem improving, I graduated high school at Fort Worth Christian in Texas with honors. For two years, I had performed well as a running back on our varsity football team where we had a strong offensive line. A lot of universities were noticing me.

Yale and Princeton University wrote to me, and I applied to both. I had graduated with honors with a 4.0 grade point average, but I didn't get in. I called the Princeton football coach and said, "Coach, I thought everything was good. I did international travel. I participated in a lot of clubs. I was president of my class, and I graduated fifth in my class. What's going on here?" He said the problem was my SAT score. "They think its a little low, and they're worried you may not be able to do the work here."

When I asked him to give me a chance, knowing that I could do it, the coach said if it was up to him he would. He recommended another option because I really wanted to go to Princeton. He suggested doing a fifth year senior year, which has helped other kids out.

After looking into it, I decided to apply to Hotchkiss, Andover, and Exeter Academy for a fifth year senior year and then attended Exeter Academy in New Hampshire. Within the first three months, I bettered my SAT score by 250 points.

While at Exeter, I started preferring Yale University over Princeton because of Yale's football coach. I reapplied to Yale, and I got in.

Mary taught me to never give up. If people don't think you're good enough, just remember that you're different in a good way. "Bryan, remember one thing: you're a contrarian." People with ADHD have a unique way of viewing the world. Many people value out-of-the-box thinking. If you ask my wife, she claims, "Bryan doesn't know where the heck the box is!"

Every problem has a solution, according to Mary. You just have to figure it out. If I can achieve, anybody can.

The first person I called up when I got into Yale University was Mary. She was such an angel in my life. I had other good teachers, but she was the one who first made me realize I had potential—which was just incredible. When I graduated from Yale University with honors, she was there.

While at Yale, I stumbled upon the fascinating subject of Jews and men of Jewish descent who served in the German military during World War II. I was intrigued. Because of my research, a lot of professors started noticing me. I began doing well in my majors, getting "As," and achieving honors.

When I was a child, a doctor had told my mom I would gravitate toward criminal activity. She was warned that kids with my learning disability get into gangs, are rebellious, get pregnant early, and do drugs. Instead of fulfilling the doctor's prophesy of my destiny, I went on to graduate from Yale with honors and received the McKim Prize for unique and groundbreaking research and also one that recognized me as the Most Improved Student at Yale University.

I was offered all three scholarships that I applied for my senior year: the Fulbright, the German Academic Exchange scholarship, and the Henry Fellowship. I accepted the Henry Fellowship from Yale, a special fellowship that allows study at Harvard, Yale, Oxford, and Cambridge.

I did my graduate study with this fellowship at Cambridge University in Darwin's College in England. I completed my master's degree and my Ph.D. The work I completed during those two degrees was the foundation for my first two books, *Hitler's Jewish Soldiers* and *Rescued from the Reich*. What's amazing is that, when I was born in 1971, in many respects, everyone thought I was the last person in the world who would to be able to read, let alone write books.

I have written three books now. My first book, called *Hitler's Jewish Soldiers*, shows readers the high number of German military men who were classified by the Nazis as Jews or "partial-Jews."

The second one, *Rescued from the Reich*, tells the story of how the U.S. government worked with the Nazi Secret Service to rescue the highest ranking Orthodox rabbi out from under the nose of the SS in World War II — an amazing rescue.

"History is a kind of introduction to more interesting people than we can possibly meet in our restricted lives; let us not neglect the opportunity."
- Dexter Perkins

Lives of Hitler's Jewish Soldiers, my third book, is a compilation of 20 of the most interesting case studies of the 2,000 I read about Jewish soldiers who fought on the side of Germany during the war. The Jewish grandfather of Helmet Schmidt, the former Chancellor of Germany, is one of them. He was in the Luftwaffe, their Air Force. Another was the "father of Blitzkrieg," three-star general, Helmet Wilberg. I was privileged to read all of his diaries and write his biography.

I was fascinated by these soldiers' lives. From my brother who was a fighter pilot to my great-great grandfather who fought in the Civil War in the Battle of Vicksburg, my family has a long military tradition. While I was finishing my Ph.D., I decided to apply to the Marines, because I thought it would be cool to fly super-sonic jets. I was 28-years-old, but the cut-off for it was 27 ½. However, they let me fly.

During my time as a Marine Corp officer, I was injured. Out of over 180,000 enlisted Marines, I was one of twelve who held a Ph.D., so I was put in a think tank, the War Fighting Lab. I organized the library and developed the personal reading list for the Marines. Half of the books that I chose I had read at Cambridge while authoring my own books.

I am proud to have been a Marine. Now, I am in the private wealth management business, and many people naturally trust me when they find out I was a Marine, because they acknowledge the work ethic — hard-working and disciplined.

Clearly, I have risen above the labels placed on me years ago by doctors and children on the playground. Parents of children who learn differently, as I did, can contact the Starpoint School at TCU, ask for literature from their pediatricians, or look to local schools to obtain information.

People with kids who learn differently must get involved. Don't be passive: be active. And learn about diet—a major key to success. Unfortunately, in America, we are digging our graves with our teeth, and we're not learning about the direct influence of these chemicals that are put in our food. They are there to extend the shelf-life of the food or to change the taste, but they are not there for your health. The more you learn about what you put in your body, the better off your mind will be.

I'm not a medical doctor, but I think medication is too often used. A lot of these drugs are like amphetamines, almost like cocaine. Some people do need medication, but too many kids are put on it because it's the easy solution. It is about popping a pill, versus transforming your lifestyle. Get educated. Get informed. Remember, these kids are not learning disabled. They are learning different.

Somebody came up to my mom recently after I gave a lecture and said, "You must be so proud!" She answered, "Yes, of course I am. I'm his mother. I'm more than proud. I'm relieved."

Bryan Mark Rigg encourages you to find out more about the Starpoint School at Texas Christian University www.coe.tcu.edu/starpoint.asp and donate to the Mary Stewart Scholarship, which honors the teacher who had a profound impact on his life.

Chapter 6

Tasha Eichenseher

Photo Credit: Tasha Eisenseher

TASHA EICHENSEHER

National Geographic has been "inspiring people to care about the planet since 1888." Tasha Eichenseher is the online environment editor and producer at National Geographic. Through her insightful journalism, she sheds light on environmental issues, exploration, and scientific discoveries globally.

I recall being on my grandfather's farm as a young child in Michigan. I spent a lot of time outside gardening and running around the prairie and the forest. I would collect plants, take them home, and press them between the pages of my journal. I'd watch my grandfather weed outside, scoop up snakes with his bare hands, and break their necks. He would throw their limp bodies out of the garden. It was at this young age that I began to see and understand the tension between man and nature.

My dad graduated from the University of Michigan with his Ph.D. in accounting, and the family ended up in Madison, Wisconsin. I was the oldest of four children. We traveled a lot internationally because my father has a fair amount of wanderlust. He took his family around the world with him. We lived in Madison the longest, but we also lived in Michigan, Illinois, and abroad in Malaysia and then Indonesia. Washington, D.C. is where I live now. Moving to different parts of the world provided a large window through which to analyze how my life compares to other people's lives.

I went to an international school in Kuala Lumpur where most of the children and families spent their weekends at the country club. But my weekends were different. Dad would take us on all sorts of trips, driving and riding the train through remote places and poor rural parts of countries.

Seeing that way of living makes you grateful for what you have. It makes you tolerant of pretty much everything. One of the hardest transitions for me was coming back my sophomore year in high school to a typical cliquish, catty environment. I think my world-view had expanded so much that I couldn't deal with that type of behavior anymore. Ironically, I actually lost my tolerance for it.

While living in Malaysia at 15-years-old, a few experiences shaped what my life is like today. Walking the streets with my family and going to some of the more wild areas of those countries (where orangutans roamed free) certainly affected how I see the world.

I had an "ah-ha" moment during a trip to the Malaysian highlands. We had been there for quite some time. I'd already seen a lot of things in the emerald green rainforest. As we drove up to the highlands, we came upon a lookout that had just been built. The asphalt was crumbling from the parking lot off the edge of the slope into the forest below. It was obviously very poorly planned. You could see all these felled trees around the site. It seemed careless to me. All of a sudden, that tension between man and nature crystallized. I was witnessing the human race's need to grow and make money clash with the environment's need to grow and support us. I've remained fascinated by this conflict and have turned that fascination into a career — writing about these issues.

I was a very serious child with a respect for nature, and I knew at that moment — watching asphalt crumble into the rainforest — that I wanted to tell stories about things that much of the world didn't know about. Fortunately, I also discovered that I have an innate ability for storytelling.

A separate trip to Sarawak, Malaysia, was a game changer that year. We did typical "tourist" things that were uncharacteristic for my family. It felt a little cheesy as we watched a cockfight and a blow-gun demonstration. On that trip, I met a woman who was a journalist for a magazine called *Tattler*. I realized then it's possible to make a career out of writing *and* traveling. I had good conversations with the journalist, and we kept in touch for a long time.

At that point in my life, I didn't feel like I had much of an outlet for my writing. I have a ridiculous number of journals that I kept as a teenager. Tons of boxes in my mother's attic are filled with them. A few years later, I was able to work for various high school publications. Then I went to college for journalism at the University of Oregon. Many years after that, I went to graduate school for environmental policy and science at the Yale School of Forestry.

In between undergrad and grad school, I fumbled in New York City for about four years, working various publishing jobs, once at a very high-profile magazine. I had a little bit of a 20-something identity crisis when I realized that I was working mostly for money at this magazine and that the content was outside the scope of what I truly cared about.

After leaving that magazine job, I made the worst financial decision of my life, though it was personally rewarding. I became an AmeriCorps volunteer. I see a lot of parallels between what I did then as an environmental educator – running literature and gardening programs out of public libraries and schools in underserved communities — and now as an environmental journalist. My original AmeriCorps contract was for just under a year, but it led to a longer-term job with an organization that advocated for clean and safe public parks.

Exposing children, and adults, to nature felt important. Just seeing kids touching an earthworm or sticking their hands in the soil to plant for the first time was pretty incredible. It's New York, an asphalt jungle. They actually thought it was cool. It was very rare that a kid wasn't interested once he or she got into the soil and started digging around. I liked being able to integrate a little more outdoor activity and science into some of their lives. I kept in touch with a couple of kids for a while after the program was over. Their parents allowed me to take them on field trips to places like the Brooklyn Botanical Garden. Getting to know who they were and how they lived was, again, another eye-opening experience, just as eye-opening as being in Malaysia or Indonesia.

From the time I was a teenager, I knew that I wanted to work at National Geographic. It combines journalism with all the subject areas that I am really interested in — travel, environment, and culture. Simply reading the magazine *National Geographic* as a child was enlightening. It made me realize that there is an audience for stories about the connections between people and the land. Plus, I have always appreciated the power of photography, and National Geographic has mastered that. I got my foot in the door at the television channel doing editorial research (one year in the states and one year in Hong Kong). Then I came back and took a job as environment editor at National Geographic's Digital Media.

It is certainly a labor of love. I don't understand the concept of having a career just to get paid. I can't imagine having a job that I didn't feel passionate about, because I spend so much time at work. I knew, because I'd always wanted to work here, it was the perfect creative outlet for me.

Working for the National Geographic Channel was challenging for various reasons. Television journalism is obviously very different from print or news journalism, which I had been accustomed to. The National Geographic Society was developed in 1888 to fund expeditions and share information from them with the rest of the world. It has grown into a multimedia business that includes the television channel, the website, the magazine, educational resources, and a huge research program. National Geographic funds hundreds of scientists in the field through several different grant programs, and my first job with the organization was to write about their findings.

Since then, the scope of my job has changed, and I now focus primarily on writing about water issues. Last year, the United Nations sponsored my travel to Nairobi, Kenya. They invited journalists globally who covered important stories about water to the United Nation's 2010 World Water Day Event. From my perspective as a journalist, just hearing from my colleagues about what it's like covering water in Uganda or the United Kingdom was very interesting.

Part of this workshop was a trip to Kibera, one of the world's largest slums, on the outskirts of Nairobi. The UN sponsors some water kiosks there with toilets, showers, and drinking water that can be utilized for a few cents. The residents of Kibera make an average of one U.S. dollar per day and do not have access to clean drinking water or sanitation services, so this is important to their village.

In Kibera, other slums, and some rural areas around the world, the sanitation problem is colossal. Close to a billion people lack adequate sanitation. That is "in your face" when you visit Kibera. I happened to go on a day when it was raining, so as I walked through the red mud streets, I got a whiff of the combination of mud and feces. I realized that I wasn't only walking through mud, but also human waste. People simply do their business on the street or they do it in a plastic bag and fling the bag somewhere, a method of waste disposal called a "flying toilet."

While in the U.S. and the rest of the developed world we have the luxury of a toilet and privacy, too much of the world suffers through this other way of living. It's my job as a journalist to bring attention to these inequalities. Because of the lack of toilets, sewage is contaminating drinking water and contributing to creation of water-borne diseases that kill nearly 1.5 million children each year.

One of the challenges in covering sanitation issues, which

> *"When we heal the earth, we heal ourselves."*
>
> *- David Orr*

I've done on and off for a few years now, is to capture the imagination or interest of people who live in the Western world and can't picture what it's really like. Being in Kibera was a fantastic chance to experience this inequality first-hand. Then I relayed to my readers what I was seeing, feeling, and smelling.

I interviewed residents of Kibera about their own experiences with the facilities that the UN had set up. But other interactions I had with people, such as sharing a laugh with a stranger about a game a kid was playing in the street, impacted my overall experience. Some people were extremely welcoming, while others were angered by my presence. My job can be intrusive, and some people may feel offended by having a reporter around. I struggle with that as a journalist; however, I'm there to tell a story.

TASHA EICHENSEHER

If I ever have the time and can collect the resources, I am interested in living in Kibera, so I would have the time to earn people's trust and to experience, on a much deeper level, what it is like to live there.

If anything can eliminate poverty and inequality, it is people feeling like they're connected to one another. A huge percentage of the world's population lives like the people of Kibera, but if people feel alienated from a part of the population, that is a fraction of the population that they don't care about. This is the same way I feel about the environment. The only way we can protect the environment is if we understand the connection we have with it. In many ways, journalism is about making connections for and with people, opening their eyes to how much we all are alike and need each other.

Why Kibera remains this way is a complicated question, just like every human rights and environmental issue. I think that, often, the poor don't have a voice in politics, so they don't have many resources coming to them to improve their situation. Stories about Kibera and other impoverished areas help shine a light on these issues.

In the truest, most stripped down sense, journalists observe and report, but what you decide to report about is subjective. As a journalist, I need to ask questions that reveal insight into difficult issues, and I need to provide critical context and arguments related to those issues, offering enough information for readers to come to their own conclusions. This is my comfort zone. That's why I think I chose this profession. I would much rather hear and tell other people's stories than tell my own.

Another reason I'm well suited for journalism is that I have a sense of adventure. I'm hungry for experiences, so I'll take them in whenever and wherever I can get them. I'm lucky that I recognized this passion early on in life. It has motivated me ever since. I think it is important to spend time trying to figure out what motivates you in life.

For children, I think it gets increasingly more difficult when they are surrounded with constant stimulation. The attention span of an average child these days is short. Television, video games, emails, texting, and smart phones are attention grabbers, making it increasingly difficult to sit still long enough to think in-depth about anything, or even read a book.

I encourage young people to turn off the TV and the computer and get outside, to find their passion and figure out how to possibly make a living out of it! You have to be adventurous and try new things to know what you like and don't like. And you have to follow your gut instinct. If you want to pursue something, try it out, and see how it feels. Be curious; curiosity is the seed for adventure. Go out, and explore until you find something that's interesting to you.

I know it's more complicated than that because all sorts of things work against exploration and curiosity these days. But all you have to do is look in your backyard or local park — you could probably find 100 different species if you took the time to look for them.

What is really cool about working at National Geographic is that, every day, I get to meet somebody new who is coming back from a trip or research project. Instead of going outside for inspiration, all I have to do is start a conversation. Sometimes, the researcher just discovered a new crazy-looking type of crab or her crew has scaled a previously unclimbed route up a huge mountain. To meet and interact with these people who are in the trenches of exploration fuels my own desire to continue to write about it.

Tasha supports the important work of the National Environmental Education Foundation (NEEF). Please go to their website — www.neefusa.org — to learn more about this organization.

Chapter 7
Clarel Radicella

Photo Credit: Pepper Negron

CLAREL RADICELLA

A strong single mother, Clarel Radicella has risen above medical obstacles, including a brain aneurysm, to inspire others, creating a web-based platform to help generate global understanding of brain-related illnesses and to promote businesses of people with disabilities. This former special education teacher shares her life lessons and her love through her story and her touching letters to her three children.

My life was meant to be different from day one. I was born in southern Africa on the beautiful tropical island of Mauritius, in the Indian Ocean. I speak French and English, as do many from my lovely, Creole birthplace.

I remember my mom telling me I was a very complicated pregnancy. Outside of the delivery room, the doctor took my dad aside and said, "She is a breech baby, and the cord is around her neck. There are multiple complications." The doctor went on to explain that only baby or mother would survive, or both of us would die during childbirth.

My mom told me that she knew in her heart that her baby was different from the start. Her baby would defy the odds. I was the first of her three girls. Everyone was amazed when I arrived in this world, healthy and strong. My mother, however, was not the least bit surprised. From a young age, she would whisper to me, "Clarel, you have a purpose."

In Mauritius, a paradise with sandy white beaches, our huge, happy extended family lived under one roof. We played outdoors together, everything from climbing trees to jumping rope. It was a totally free and simple life.

I recall spending hours in a lush garden with my grandfather. Lying on my belly in the thick grass, I read books as he pruned his beautiful, abundant flowers, pointing out each type to me.

The delicate white muguet blossomed like mini-wedding bells. I envisioned the colorful bird of paradise flowers taking flight. There in Grandpa's tropical garden, I soaked in stories from novels and from my grandfather about his World War II days. In that breathtaking setting, I learned how difficult times like war could build character. Lost in our conversations, he passed on stories about how people can better themselves and taught me how to appreciate differences and find commonalities in people.

When we came to America, my parents worked with the United Nations: my father side-by-side with diplomats and ambassadors, while my mother worked in Human Resources. My sisters and I were enrolled in the United Nations International School in New York City, an amazing school brimming with diversity and culture. Despite the language barriers, communication was still possible. As young students in this setting, we realized that so much existed beyond our little world. Just looking at our friends' faces and hearing their accents, we knew more was out there to explore. It makes you want to see and be more. As a family, we often visited other families in different parts of the world. I realized even then that I had an incredible life. My horizons were broadened as I experienced Portugal, France, Italy, and Africa, all before graduating from high school.

I was privileged to grow up in this globally rich setting. Now, fast forward a few decades.

I was forty years old and had just gone through a divorce. I felt fulfilled being a special education teacher and free to start anew with my life. I was capable and strong in knowing who I was. I had family and friends to support me who were always going to be there for me. I felt good.

One evening, I was having dinner with my eight-year-old daughter Christina, singing along to American Idol, when I realized I couldn't feel my left side. Something was wrong. I thought maybe my leg had just fallen asleep, but when I tried to lift my left arm, it didn't move. I realized that I was half-paralyzed.

I told Christina to call 911 right away, to unlock the door, and open it so the paramedics could get in. Then, we called her grandparents and father.

The next thing I knew, I was in the ambulance speeding towards the emergency room, and my condition was worsening. I could no longer speak. I could only shake my head to respond "yes" or "no" and point with my working hand. Finally at the hospital, I was checked by a doctor who called for an MRI and a CAT scan immediately. I was really scared.

I was diagnosed with an arteriovenous malformation (AVM), a rare brain disorder that causes an atypical connection between the arteries and veins. It functions as a mass like a tumor, causing me to experience neurological deficits such as the partial paralysis.

A year after the paralysis, I drove myself to the emergency room because I had the worst headache I ever felt. In excruciating pain, I abandoned my car randomly in the lot.

This time, I was diagnosed with a brain aneurysm on the opposite side of the brain from my AVM. The hospital staff was shocked that I was able to drive myself there. They said that I had saved my life by getting to the hospital so quickly and I was fortunate to even have survived the drive.

While I was fortunate to make it there safely, I had more news to come regarding my overall health. Unfortunately, all the doctors could say was, "The AVM and aneurysm combination is inoperable. We can't do anything. We cannot help you."

I am a single mom with three kids. I wanted to keep teaching school. I had a life to live. I remember thinking, "Do I accept that my days are numbered? Can I push forward?" I had so much to fight for!

In 2005, after I got the news, I had to stop teaching. It was a painful goodbye with my students. The principal was so respectful of my needs. My last week of teaching, she had three extra people in the room to help me. She even encouraged me to invite a family member in to see what I was like as a teacher. I chose the one person who I knew would see the true essence of who I was. I chose my dear mother. Mom was totally mesmerized, watching me connect with the special needs children. I'm thankful that she could be there.

I felt so fragile at the time. There I was, teaching kids with learning disabilities, developmental disabilities, ADHD, and autism, yet I was learning to live with a disability myself during those days. I treasured my last moments with them.

Once I was settled into the hospital, I received cards from every one of my students. Those cute little people who struggled daily in the classroom remembered Mrs. Radicella (or "Mrs. R" to most of them) and our bond. The principal read each card aloud by my hospital bed, as I shut my eyes and soaked in their sweet words.

I realized at that point that it was my turn to be the student and learn quickly, to learn more about life, myself, and two illnesses. It was not easy to accept that a part of me was changing so drastically.

I was assigned a caseworker, who promptly asked me what I planned on telling my kids to prepare them for my death. I told her that was not why she was there. Then came her million-dollar question, "What can I do to help you?" That was it. Little did she know the forest fire of determination she had just sparked in my mind. My upcoming learning process — learning to adjust to no longer working with my students and to my drastic life changes — would be therapeutic. More importantly though, I needed her help to find the resources to heal me. "I don't want to just forget about life."

Deep in my heart, I knew I was going to persevere but that I needed to find a place that would take my special case: the right people to take care of me. "Do you really want to do this?" she asked. "It's going to take time that you may not have. You don't even know if there is such a place." But I knew I had to do it. I thought about my children. I wasn't ready to give up.

For two years, we researched hospitals and support groups. Finally, we thought UPMC in Pittsburgh, PA looked promising. Trusting it would work, I acted on my gut feeling and referred myself as a patient. When a nurse answered the phone, I explained, "I have received care in my hometown, but we have not been successful. I have been kicked to the curb and left to die. I am not ready to give up!"

She immediately transferred me to the neurosurgeon, Dr. Horowitz. When I described to him what was happening, he told me to get my paperwork together and come see him in two weeks. He said, "It is going to be a long road, but we will take care of you. Don't worry about anything right now. You just be the patient. We will figure everything else out."

At UMPC Pittsburgh, I met Dr. Munsford and had gamma knife surgery, during which they injected six-months-worth of radiation therapy directly into my brain. The doctors and other staff there were incredible, so positive, never once doubting. That medical team has been there for me. Every six months, I go back for the treatment, completely trusting them with my life.

I was finally getting healthy, putting the weight back on that I had lost. Only ten percent of the AVM was left, and the aneurysm had been repaired. I was successfully being treated, and I was on my way to being well.

The next and last surgery for my brain would have been in the summer of 2011, but I had a detour. I guess you could say that I took the scenic route to my final appointment. Heartbreakingly, it was not the stunning scenery of my grandfather's lush tropical gardens. Instead, the detour looped around a word that no one wants to hear.

In late December 2010, every time I ate or drank, I would feel queasy. Again, I started losing weight. All the while, I was working hard on my website and networking through social media. With the help of my friend Cassandra Allen, I was getting "Mind Your Business" (www.mindyourbiz.org) up and running to spread the word around the world about AVM and aneurysms while promoting businesses of people with disabilities. Though I was productive, I began to feel worse and worse. I went to the doctor after I couldn't eat my mother's delicious Christmas dinner. I was sure something was wrong. After all, she can really cook!

The hospital ran a couple tests that showed it clearly wasn't something I ate or a virus. Finally, the doctor recommended a more sophisticated diagnostic tool: an endoscopy done by a gastrointestinal specialist. I thought this was going to be a minor setback in my health. Instead, I got the surprise of my life.

Frowning, the doctor said, "That picture doesn't look too good." I asked to see the pictures, unable to imagine what could be wrong. Even though they felt they should wait for my office visit, they brought them in for me in the recovery room. I have always been the straightforward type of patient: "What does the report say?" "How are we going to fix it?" The doctor revealed that I had multiple tumors inside my stomach.

Waiting at home for the results of the biopsy, I felt even worse and went to the emergency room. It was then I was finally told that I had stomach cancer and needed surgery. It was insanely fast the way it happened. I had a part of my stomach removed, and the next thing I knew, I was recovering from the painful procedure. The surgeon got me really good, too – lots of cuts!

Two days later, though, I received a phone call from the hospital telling me my lymph nodes were cancerous as well. They needed to open me up and get right back in there. Imagine being told over the phone, "You are going to have your second surgery for cancer in two hours. Hurry back to the hospital."

My best friend Evin was by my side. He has been there for every single surgery. The doctor told us what the procedure would entail. Basically, they had to remove pieces and redesign the entire digestive system to get rid of all the cancer that was there. They also needed to make sure that when the surgery was over, I would be left with a body that could function on its own in spite of all the major changes.

They told me to surround myself with my family. I knew this was going to be a tough one, and I made as many phone calls as I could. Friends and family gathered around me. As each person walked in, I urged them to pray. After that, everything is a blur. I just wanted to make it through.

After the five-and-a-half-hour-long surgery, I woke up in a tremendous amount of pain, but I was so happy. Everyone there was praying for me to pull through, and encouraging me with their presence. I cheered in my head, "I am here! I am alive!"

I have been so close to the other side before. Three times I have flat-lined and the paddles were used on me. I know what it feels like to experience the white light of that energy. It is a sensation of having no pain and such beautiful peace. To go through that, survive, and then meet other people who have gone through similar experiences is incredible.

When I flatlined, just like in the movies, I could see the doctors working on me as I was in the operating room. I journeyed to different rooms and saw friends and family members. I could see what they were doing. Not only that, but when I later told them what I saw them doing, they surprisingly confirmed that what I said was true. Now, the only time I can feel anything slightly similar is when I meditate and feel spiritually connected on all levels. You have to know how to intensely meditate to get even close to that level of serenity.

Lately, the pain has been unbearable. Painkillers, including morphine, barely dull it. Only one thing works: the power of the mind. I must be able to get up each day, no matter how much pain I am experiencing.

Not even a day after the surgery, the nurses said, "This is going to be the toughest thing you are going to do. You need to stand up and walk out of your room. Go down the hall with all of those stitches in your belly. If you can make that long walk, you are going to be OK."

I sternly said, "Help me get out of bed. I am not waiting a day or two days. I am going to get this done right now." I knew that my feet would touch that ground and I would walk. My nurses, one on my right side and one on my left, prepared me for the pain I was going to feel. I walked right through the pain. Not just to the point in the hallway they set as my goal. Oh no, I had a better goal. I wanted to go past the doors.

One door was half-closed, and one door was open. "You see that open one?" I said. "That's the one I want to go through." To their astonishment, I did just that. I walked past that half-closed door, through the open door and gained my mental and physical freedom. I took myself to that next level. It was then that I knew I was going to be alright. I did it for myself so I could find new strength.

I thought I knew what strength was after the AVM and aneurysm. I didn't. Cancer is whole different ballgame. It is unbearable pain. I read in a book once that, "to be able to overcome the pain is to be able to overcome the medical condition." I always wondered exactly what that meant before I got cancer. Now, I understand it. If you can harness the power of your mind and get past the pain, you know you can make it.

Now, spring of 2011, I have had my latest two surgeries and am healing, waiting a couple of weeks before the next treatment. In the meantime, I get to have some fun. My beautiful oldest daughter is getting married the first weekend of May. It's going to be awesome because the whole family will be together in the city at the hotel, celebrating from the minute that we can start. The wedding will be in Central Park in New York and then we will all spend Mother's Day together.

The whole weekend was planned prior to everyone knowing that I was ill again, so the extended time together wasn't because of my illness. We have always valued the importance of family togetherness and quality moments.

In a few weeks, I will start radiation, but without much chemo. The doctors are optimistic about my case. Sometimes I feel weak and frustrated, and I have a little pity party. But other times I remember it's just pain, and pain is temporary.

My mindset, however, is not temporary. Except for minor lapses of strength, I am always positive. Since the beginning of my life, I have been a little fighter. I am a survivor. I can pull through anything. I will make the best of it. I am going forward with my business plan. I am working with Ray Leonard and Dr. Shellie Hipsky on this powerful book. We will be expanding the website to include cancer support. I will reach my goals.

Right now, my children are 26, 20, and 16 years old. As a mom, it is such an emotional issue to talk about my health with my kids. I wish they didn't have to go through it. I want them to see me healthy. They do realize even after all I have gone through, Mommy doesn't just sit in bed all day. She is still doing the "Mind Your Business thing" and still networking.

If you ever end up this sick, you cannot let yourself have a pity party and just sit around. Find the energy to do something positive. You will feel so much better, and better able to cope with the sickness.

When I do let myself sulk, it just makes me feel worse. It's not worth it! Yes, it does suck, and it's natural to cry about it. Be honest with others. Get it out of your system. Most importantly, pray. Not everyone is spiritual, but I feel that everyone does it one way or another through an inner-conversation.

I would rather it be me than a friend or family member going through this. At least I have the capability to help myself heal by maintaining a positive attitude.

Don't doubt your strength or the power of the mind. Never feel that you are alone. I remember being in my hospital bed in the middle of the night crying, when a nurse walked in, and without speaking a word, she just held my hand. It showed me love and compassion. Touch has a lot to do with healing. Studies have shown that babies who are touched thrive, while babies who are ignored don't grow as well. If you touch a sick baby or child, they soon thrive; they blossom. It is the same way with adults who are disabled or who have illnesses. It stimulates them. They feel loved, and it recharges their desire to live. I want to be able to show and teach others about the power of touch.

If you come to see me, please hold my hand, give me a hug, and show me you care. I cannot stress enough the power of touch to heal and make things better.

Yesterday, I was feeling so down. When my mom came in, I asked her to just hold my hand. Once she did that simple act, I felt much better. Just touching my forehead and holding my hand made it all better. I show this same compassion to my children. It doesn't matter how big they are. Every day I say, "I love you." I cherish hugging them every single time I see them.

CLAREL RADICELLA

I want to leave messages for each of my three amazing children. They know in their hearts that I love them, but this book gave me an opportunity for my children to have a piece of me to cling to whenever they need their Mommy. Here are the notes to my darling children ...

Jennifer, 26 my oldest daughter:

My Jennifer,
Oh, Sweetie. When I think about you, I admire how laid back you are and how you deal with things in life. Wow, you have taught me a lot about peace of mind. What you have shown me is how to take it easy and accept things for what they are. Sometimes you get frustrated, and you say it like it is, but nonetheless, you let it roll off your shoulders, and you just keep moving. You don't dwell on yesterday because you are always looking forward to tomorrow, knowing that today may not be great, all the while, realizing that there is a tomorrow. You are "incredible" in every sense of the word. That is what you have taught me, Jennifer: That today might be ok or it might not be all that great, yet, that is what tomorrows are for . . . to make them even better than today.

Hugs,
Mom

Cyrus, my 20-year-old son:

Dear Cyrus,
You showed me what a man should be: a real man. That love and compassion go hand-in-hand. I learned from you, that sometimes you have to put your differences aside and continue to love people no matter what or who they are. You have taken time out to let Mommy realize that even though things are not always perfect, that I can't be around all the time, and that I am very sick, it's about the quality of the time we have spent together. In

spite of it all, you let me know that even though I am not always feeling good, it is "all good." I am not always healthy, but in your eyes, I am fine and perfect as a mom. I couldn't ask for anything more.
Love,
Mommy

Christina, my 16-year-old daughter who I call "Bina," which is short for the Italian word "bambina," which means "baby":

Darling Christina,
My Bina, you have seen me sick since you were only eight years old. Mommy loves you so much. I have learned from you what it means to be strong and spiritual. You don't give up or give in. You have the heart of a warrior. Right now, you are a stubborn, rebellious teenager. I am glad you have shown me these character traits, which are perfectly natural for teenagers, because this is a time in my life that I need to know that you are going to be alright. Even though you cry, it is not just because you are sad. Sometimes it's because you are watching me try so hard. You have said to me, "Mom, where do you get the strength from?" Honey, I get it from you. I see that you are only 16, you are ambitious, and you don't give up. You are who I am learning it from. Thank you.

With Love,
Mommy

All three of my children, I learn from daily. In the midst of the chaos, we will share a beautiful wedding. There will be graduations and birthdays. We always have plenty to celebrate. We are going to keep going. You just watch.

Someday, I will be in my heavenly garden in the sky back with my Grandpa. My legacy lives on through my children. It will keep going on and on as they get married and have families of their own. One day, they will pass our shared experiences on to the next generation. My grandfather taught me to pass my love and knowledge on, and I am doing so with this book and my actions. I will continue the fight, just as I did as a baby, because my mother was correct: I have a purpose.

Please support Clarel Radicella's Mind Your Business website, which promotes e-commerce for all supporting businesses, owners and entrepreneurs, non-profits, and other causes, with an emphasis on those who are disabled. Also, learn more about how you can help Clarel and others with AVMs, brain aneurysms, and cancer at www.mindyourbiz.org.

Chapter 8

Sandie Andersen

Left: Annamarie Ausnes   Right: Sandie Andersen

SANDIE ANDERSEN

You reach the front of the line at Starbucks. You know what you want. "A Cinnamon Dolche-skim milk extra hot-no whip," a "Triple Venti non-fat latte," or a "Cafe Mocha Grande with whipped cream, extra half and half, and two Splenda." Whatever your order, you have probably never asked for or received a body organ. Annamarie Ausnes has. Sandie Andersen, a Starbuck's barista, donated her kidney to her customer who then turned into a dear friend. *O, The Oprah Magazine* **included Sandie in an article titled "Ladies First: 34 Women from History Who Dared to Change the World," and CNN filmed a documentary on the kidney exchange.**

I'm a barista at 26 and Procter in Tacoma, Washington. I have worked in this family-friendly neighborhood for seven years. I've been married for 25 years. We have three daughters and three grandkids. I live pretty simply. We have a little house in Tacoma, and I work part-time so I can be here for my grandkids when they get home after school. I'm 55 – and I'm a young 55, let me tell you. I'm in good shape.

My husband works a couple doors down from me. That's why I chose that store, because he can come over and have coffee with me in the mornings. I really like him, even after 25 years.

Because I work early (4 o'clock in the morning), I get all the people who are on their way to work. They don't want to talk because they just got up. But, I know their drinks. They're in, and they're out. We call it a "commuter store" because they're leaving their homes and heading for the freeway into Seattle. I don't really get to know their names. Instead, I get to know their likes and dislikes; its the little things you pick up on from people who are half-asleep when they walk in the door.

Over the years, you get to know people. You have their coffee ready, ring them up, and they're out the door. One customer who I knew was a "short-drip double cup," came in every day, but I didn't know her name. I found out she had grandkids in California, because I asked her where she went when she'd be away and come back tan.

She was usually just a regular, nice person. Then she started coming in and not saying very much. She would get a small coffee or a water and didn't seem to be doing well.

You can tell by people's body language when they walk in there if they've had a good night's sleep or a bad night's sleep, or if something is going on with them. You definitely can tell.

It was a gloomy, rainy day when I noticed the change in her. She told me she had "health issues." Well, there are many types of health issues. I wanted to know what kind, because I figured that maybe I could do something. I like to give. I'm involved in my community, in my kids' schools, and in my grandkids' schools.

> *"I have found that among its other benefits, giving liberates the soul of the giver."*
> *- Mother Teresa*

She said she was getting a fistula – connecting a couple of blood vessels in her arm – for dialysis, and she needed a kidney. It didn't look too promising. Her family and friends were not matches.

There she was standing in Starbucks telling me that she's going to die if she didn't get a kidney, and I thought to myself that I could help. I said, "You know what? I'm going to get the test and see if I am match for you." We were so excited about our little conversation that she pulled out a business card from the hospital, wrote down her blood-type, and forgot to write down her name or phone number. She handed me the card and walked out the door.

All I kept thinking was that I had to get my blood tested to see if our blood types matched. I called my doctor afterwards, and he told me to come in the next morning. I got my blood tested, waited the next day, and didn't hear anything, so I called the hospital. They said they would send me a packet to see if this was something I would really be interested in. When the packet arrived, I went through it and filled out a whole bunch of paperwork. Five days after they processed the paperwork, I found out that I was a match.

Don't get me wrong, there were points when I had to wonder what I had just committed to doing. After all, I am a human being. On the other hand, I felt like it was a little bigger than me. I have very strong faith, and I just felt in my gut that this was something I was supposed to do. Then, I had to convince the rest of my family.

When I told my husband, he was eating spaghetti for dinner. That probably wasn't a great choice timing-wise to tell him. I blurted out, "You know honey, I'm thinking about giving a kidney to a customer." And he said, "Well, who?" Then I said, "I don't know." He kind of choked a bit on his dinner. Then I explained the situation, and he just looked at me like he was hoping this was just a phase.

When we got the information from the hospital, I knew that once he was more educated on the situation, he would be on-board with me. That was exactly the case.

I had decided that I would do it, and my family was supporting me. The only trick? I didn't even know the woman's name.

I went back to work and was asking everybody, "Does anyone know who the 'short-drip double cup' is?" I knew it seemed crazy. They kept asking me why I wanted to know.

Finally, after about a week, she came walking in the door, and I was at the register. I was fired up in anticipation. I was going to grab her and tell her I was going to do this for her. The line was to the door, and I was ready to explode. When she got up to the counter, I grabbed her hands and started crying my eyes out as I said, "I'm going to give you a kidney."

She started crying. The people in line were rolling their eyes because they wanted their coffees. They didn't know that a life-changing moment had just happened. It was pretty amazing.

My friends at work were all around me in tears, saying, "That sounds like you!" I think they thought at first it was just a crazy idea that wasn't really going to go through.

The next day I met with Annamarie for three hours, and we got to know each other. Then I sat down with my family to do a family history and figure out if it was going to be smart for me to go through with it. After all, if your kid needs a kidney later on, you would feel pretty awful if you gave one to a stranger! We did a lot of research for the next few weeks.

Every time I went to the hospital for another test, the results showed I was a better and better match. It took three months of extensive testing. They want to make sure you're a sane, healthy person who's doing it for the right reasons.

> *"You don't have to be an angel, just be someone who can give."*
> *- Patti LaBelle*

I was on a walk with my daughter when they finally called and said, "It's a go. You are a perfect match for Annamarie. Do you want to call her?" It was the end of February, and the surgery was set for March 11th. I started crying, so my daughter was wondering what was wrong. Then I told her, and she teared up as well.

Immediately, I called Annamarie. We were both on the telephone standing on the corner outside next to our houses jumping up and down, because her life was going to be saved.

It's an incredible thing. I had never done anything really sacrificial, except maybe not getting enough sleep. It was a pretty exciting feeling.

We were in the same surgery room with just a wall between us. I went in about three hours ahead of her.

We had different reactions physically to the surgery while we healed in separate rooms. They said that within 30 seconds of putting that kidney in her, her original kidneys quit working and mine started. They don't think mine had a chance to know that it was in a different body.

When I got out of surgery, I woke up thinking, "What truck hit me?" I was a little confused while I was coming out of the anesthesia because I knew I was healthy before I went in for surgery.

Annamarie went in very, very sick, and when she came out of surgery, she was full of life. She talked to everybody and was wide awake. She was doing extremely well.

The most touching moment was when her 22-year-old son Scotty walked down to my room and stood in the doorway with tears running down his face. He was this big football player-type of guy, and he whispered, "All I can say is, 'thank you.'" That was pretty darn touching.

When I was able to get up, they helped me and all of my equipment to roll down to her room. Annamarie and I spent a few hours crying and talking.

There was a lot of local media attention at the time of the surgery, because we were strangers when I made the decision to help her. Bigger media outlets got a hold of the story, and CNN even filmed the kidney exchange and did a documentary on it

Now we're amazing friends. That's what is so awesome. We both have grandkids, and we both love to travel, so we've been going on vacation together. You know, I gave her a new life, but she gave me back an amazing friendship. I sign everything, "One less kidney, but a very full heart."

We just celebrated the three-year anniversary of the surgery by giving each other yellow roses of friendship. We call them our "Kidney Roses." She was so sick before. Now, she is having a blast spending time with her grandchild, and her daughter is getting married. It's a great story with a happy ending!

Donate Life is a national charity that I support. To be a donor while you are alive, you have to be really, really healthy, and you have to have a good mindset. It's something just about everyone can do. Dialysis can only extend a person's life five to seven years. A kidney from a cadaver can only extend a person's life about seven years. But a kidney from a live donor, should take Annamarie into her old age, and I get to watch her live a full, healthy life.

Recently, a little man who was in his 70s came into Star-bucks. He waited and waited until everyone was gone, and then he said, "I saw you on TV. I got something because of you." It turns out, someone was inspired by our story, and knowing this man was on dialysis, the person had given him a kidney. He smiled as he handed me a little box, saying, "I have something for you that you gave up." Inside was a pretty sterling silver kidney on a chain.

Go out, and do something good! It is so worth it. Even if you donate blood or bone marrow or just do something kind for someone, you don't know how good it's going to make you feel inside. After all, why are we on this planet if not for each other?

Donate Life, Inc., is a 501(c)(3)non-profit organization dedicated to changing the reality of those who wait for life-saving organ transplants through a direct campaign of education and awareness. To learn more about Donate Life, go to www.donatelife.org.

Chapter 9

Shannon McNamara

Photo Credit: Karen Hill McNamara

SHANNON MCNAMARA

In 2008 at just 15, Shannon McNamara founded SHARE, Shannon's After-school Reading Exchange, a non-profit literacy program for girls in rural Tanzania. She received the Outstanding Youth Achievers' Recognition at the 7th Annual Youth Assembly at the United Nations for this project. Following this, Shannon was honored with many other accolades for her work empowering African girls through education, including the 2010 Gloria Barron Prize for Young Heroes, the 2010 National Prudential Spirit of the Community Award, the 2010 New Jersey State Governor's Jefferson Award, and the Girl Scouts of the USA 2010 National Young Woman of Distinction. She represented the United Nations' Girl Up campaign in her speech given at the White House. Through SHARE, she mobilized 900 teens to volunteer thousands of hours collecting and boxing 33,000 books, which were shipped to Africa.

First off, I want to go on record saying *Jersey Shore*, *The Real Housewives of New Jersey*, and *Jerseylicious* do not represent what all girls from Jersey are like. I am from New Jersey, and I started an organization—SHARE—to educate girls in another part of the world. I chose SHARE's motto, "Today a reader, Tomorrow a leader," to inspire these young women to achieve.

Many girls who attend the primary schools in East Africa struggle to become literate. On top of a lack of resources, they are expected to perform household chores such as fetching water barefoot from five miles away, a task that takes valuable time away from their studies. SHARE is dedicated to addressing this problem by empowering girls in Africa through education. We have been able to set up four school libraries in Tanzania and have also supplied books to our partner organizations in South Africa, Malawi, and Zanzibar, benefiting 8,000 students and teachers.

Empowering young women in Africa is very exciting. The fact is, education can bring out confidence and encourage these girls. It is incredible to watch something like that happen. Just being able to read a book makes these girls so much more willing to share their ideas and explore new possibilities. People need to recognize that books have the amazing power to change lives.

I am 18 years old now, but the foundation for starting my organization began when I was a kid. As I was growing up, my parents kept reminding me that I won the "birth lottery of life," because I could have just as easily been a girl born in Africa where I'd have to spend all day fetching water and firewood, and caring for my siblings. I was lucky to be born in this country, where I could go to school and eventually use my voice and potential to help other people.

Giving back and volunteering were values my parents instilled in me. And now I know it's the right thing for me to do. I think everyone should volunteer. It is so rewarding.

My family lived in Ireland and New Zealand, as well as the United States, while I was growing up. We also took several international trips on holidays. After a few years, we realized that we weren't being immersed in the culture of these places: we were interfacing with the tourist industry. That was the main reason we started seeking out "volunteer vacations." My family would spend a few weeks in a developing country working in an orphanage, school, or old-age home together. We enjoyed learning about a different culture first-hand and working together as a family. You get the "helper's high" when you repair and paint a room or talk with the girls and share cross-cultural information. All five of us were hooked.

Our love for traveling makes our volunteering that much more rewarding. I've volunteered in Peru and Costa Rica with my family, and in India with the Girl Scouts of the USA. For the past three summers, my family has been going back to Africa. My brother and sister have been to China. My mom and my sister have been to Guatemala. We try to go wherever we possibly can to help people.

In 2008, I traveled to Africa and was amazed how some-body could live on so little. "Africa-poor" is different from "Peru-poor" or "Costa Rica-poor." Sub-Saharan Africa ranks at the bottom of all developing countries economically, due to lack of resources and harsh living conditions. People who live there are grateful for the tiniest thing, even a pencil. This was when I realized that I had the potential to change their lives.

"Any book that helps a child to form a habit of reading, to make reading one of his deep and continuing needs, is good for him."
- Maya Angelou

Because I had been to other developing countries—Peru, Costa Rica, and India—I had less travel shock with Africa, and I knew not to assume what people need but to *ask* them what they need. Communication with the people you are helping is one of the most important things.

On one of our last days at the school we had been work-ing with on our first trip to Africa, the head mistress pulled my mom and me aside, saying "Don't forget us." You could see in her eyes that other people had just dropped off money or sup-plies and then left. I didn't want to be one of those people, doing my good deed for the day, and never returning. I was moved by her plea and knew I could do something more. That was a deciding factor for us. As a family we were going to con-tinue with the project because these girls meant so much to us. This was when I started SHARE in Africa, in 2008, when I was 15 years old.

When we started SHARE, we got a list of all the needs in the community, which made the people there feel like somebody was finally listening to them. The list mostly dealt with health issues (like AIDs) and educational issues (including books, computers, classrooms, pencils, and pens). You can accomplish so much more working together with the people you are trying to help.

We sent out fliers, brochures, and little messages after our summer there to people in our lives. Generous friends, members of our family, and neighbors dropped off books, school supplies, and even some old laptops. Since then, the donations have been flowing in to SHARE. However, right now we're not collecting books, anymore because we've already shipped down a lot and it's expensive to keep shipping.

In the near future, we plan on piloting a program so the girls can have access to more books on e-readers, which will reduce shipping costs. In fact, when I went on the nationally televised program "The Nate Berkus Show" the host jumpstarted our e-reader movement for the girls of Tanzania.

Storage is tricky. Our family had to clean out the garage, basement, and the rest of the house to store donations. Obviously, my parents are both big supporters. I have an incredible mom, an awesome family, and numerous volunteers who are dedicated to this cause. It wouldn't be possible without them, not only because of what they do but also because of their support. That's what makes this not seem like work. It's wonderful that I have everybody helping me with this goal. I am fortunate to be able to give back like this.

During our first summer visit, I saw how grateful the girls were for things that we take for granted every day. Before we brought pencils and other school supplies, if you saw a child with a pencil, she would break it into three pieces to share it with her friends so they would all have something to write with, because supplies are so limited in Africa.

Another time during that trip, we passed around a Costco-sized box of Shredded Mini-Wheats, as a snack for all the SHARE girls. If you pass around a box of food in America, people will take a handful for themselves, but each girl instead took just one from the box. I saw some of the girls tucking the Shredded Mini-Wheat inside their pockets to bring home to share with somebody in the family.

The second summer of the program, my family dropped in on the school a day early to see for ourselves if the program was working. My brother videotaped us as we approached the school. Because it was quiet, we assumed they weren't there, and we were disappointed that the program might not be working. Then we noticed shoes sitting outside the door. We entered the classroom to see many girls busily studying and working in silence. To my delight, they sang a song and honored me with an impromptu ceremony. It was incredible!

When we came back the second summer, we were happy to see that the girls were much more confident, looking us in the eye and having conversations with us, after a year of the SHARE program and a better education. We passed around a box of Shredded Wheat again, but they took handfuls that time. That showed just how much their confidence had grown.

SHARE held a parents' meeting during our first summer to entice the parents to let their daughters join the program. At first, a couple of the parents declined, saying they needed their daughters at home cooking and cleaning.

> *"If you can't feed a hundred hungry people, feed just one."*
> *-Mother Teresa*

It broke my heart to see that some of these girls wouldn't be in the program because their parents didn't understand the long-term benefits of education. However, many of the mothers did understand and appreciated the opportunity. One with a baby on her back said to me, "Thank you for helping my daughter!" You could see the gratitude in her eyes.

Many people want to get involved in helping out their neighborhood, the country, or the world but are not sure where to turn. Check out some websites or Facebook pages to learn about the non-profits in your area, nationally, or globally and just take the plunge. It may be hard to take that first step, but once you take it, you feel great, and the rest is history.

My high school friends are extremely supportive of what I do and help to spread the word. I remember once, during track practice a freshman guy who I'd never talked to before asked me if I was "the girl with all the books." I answered, "Yep, that's me. I'm the girl with all the books." I'm excited that everybody knows about it.

I always get Facebook messages from people saying, "I want to help out! What can I do?" Or, "I have my own project, could you help me with some ideas for it?" So many people have been able to get involved in SHARE, and other people have been inspired by SHARE to start their own projects about things that they feel passionate about. I love that.

I am proud of the recognition that SHARE has received. I was awarded the United Nations Youth Achievement Recognition Award in New York in 2010. The week-long conference beforehand was incredible. I was able to attend meetings and speeches where I met other people who were doing philanthropic projects. I also learned about other ways to help SHARE, whether it was through social media, promotion, or making connections. Simply hearing about others with high-impact projects was inspiring. I was honored to receive the award, and it benefitted my work because I heard people from around the world give speeches on what they had done to improve lives. The best part was being able to meet so many other people who are inspired by the same causes.

Then on the day I received the award, I was actually standing on the stage where only people who were given this recognition had stood. It was a great experience.

Now, people in the public eye are taking notice of the SHARE projects, such as Nigel Barker, Miley Cyrus, and Condoleezza Rice. SHARE doesn't have a "celebrity spokesperson" yet, but with celebrities at least supporting us, word should spread more quickly about the benefits of the program.

Oprah Winfrey's radio show and website featured SHARE, and she highlighted me as an exceptional female in March 2009. It was so cool because everybody knows Oprah! When I became a part of Oprah's Angel Network, I began to see the power of social media and what it could mean for SHARE.

The most amazing experience I had since starting SHARE was when Michelle Obama invited me to speak at the White House on March 8, 2011 to celebrate the 100th anniversary of International Women's Day. I discussed the importance of empowering girls in developing countries and why girls in this country must reach out to girls around the world.

I am always looking to the future of SHARE in Africa. Currently, we are launching our newest program called "SHARE Scholars" which provides scholarships to SHARE girls in our primary schools to attend the Hekima Girls' Secondary School, an exceptional boarding school, for four years.

The main reason Hekima was chosen is because it is one of the leading schools in the region. The girls pass their national exams and do very well. Hekima is the only all-girls private secondary school in this region, and they purposefully enroll some orphans to provide them shelter and teach them self-reliance.

Although the girls work hard in school, some of them can't continue their education because their parents simply don't have the money to pay for it. With SHARE Scholars, we could sponsor them for another four years, so they have an option other than getting married young. Instead, they can improve their education and have more opportunities.

Currently, 95% of girls in Tanzania do not graduate high school! Once they are educated they can go on to be teachers and nurses. Some run their own business or become more efficient farmers. It is the way it was in the USA years ago. There is a lot of gender discrimination in Tanzania.

Sometimes they graduate and go on to raise their families. As educated mothers they often have fewer children and are more passionate about educating those children, especially the girls. Literate mothers can educate and read to their children. Also, her children are healthier, due to little things like being able to read the words on the medicine bottle for the children when they are sick.

Most importantly, an educated woman in Tanzania can earn money to support her family. This is huge. A woman in Sub-Saharan Africa typically reinvests 90% of her income into her family. A man there invests just 35% into his family's household. Many men there spend their money on banana beer, sugary drinks, and other nasty habits. Women don't. They spend it on things like food, school fees, and clothing for their children. As the African proverb states, "If you educate a man you educate an individual, but if you educate a woman you educate a family."

The success of our SHARE program in Africa has encouraged me to eventually open SHARE chapters in India, China, and Chile. The future looks promising for SHARE and the girls who take advantage of the program. I have been lucky to see first-hand how a book can make a difference.

To suport Shannon in her mission to help African girls become the leaders of tomorrow, please see the video, tweets, articles, and how to contribute at SHARE, Shannon's After-school Reading Exchange www.shareinafrica.org or "like" SHARE's Facebook page.

Ordinary People Extraordinary Planet

Chapter 10

Qun Queeney Tang

QUN QUEENEY TANG

Qun Queeney Tang was a Cardiologist in China for ten years after studying Internal Medicine at Shanghai Second Medical University. She is now an Emerald Director at USANA Health Sciences, Inc. and the CEO of Newlife Health Science, Inc. in Pittsburgh, PA, where she manages thousands of people and speaks around the world about health issues. She works hard to spread information about wellness, diet, supplements, and exercise, globally.

Curled up on a lab table in the hospital, I laid down for just a second to take a nap. I knew I had to get up moments later to rush back down the hall to my cardiac patients. I was constantly working; in just half a year on the job after earning my doctorate, I had analyzed almost 2,000 patients' blood samples. My body was getting sick. Constantly nauseated and utterly exhausted, I knew I couldn't continue this crazy pace forever. I was working such long hours that, even though I wanted to spend time with my young son, I had to send him to a residential school so he would be cared for properly. There were simply not enough hours in the day.

While I was working these incredibly long hours that were wearing me down, one of my colleagues came to me, upset about a parking ticket he just got. My friend was bothered that the policeman who gave him the ticket was very angry. Complaining of a headache that afternoon, he went home early. By evening, he fell into a coma and was brain dead. Three days later, this smart, young doctor with a Ph.D. from England died at 31 years old. He left us forever.

If you do not take care of your emotional and physical health, you may experience sub-health. Sub-health, also called "the third state," is a mid-point between unhealthy conditions or disease and healthy conditions. Sleep or appetite issues, heart palpitations, head- or body-aches, and emotional issues such as anxiety or depression are signs of sub-health. Some serious patients struggle with working and studying or suffer from low self-esteem with no desire for progress or loss of memory or the ability to concentrate.

A global investigation by the World Health Organization (WHO) determined that only 5% of the world's population enjoys actual "good health"; 20% have an illness, after investigation and diagnosis; but up to 75% are in the sub-health condition. I realized that the stress of my job was deeply affecting me, and I no longer had good health.

Realizing I needed to make a positive change for my family and myself, we moved to Vancouver, Canada. When I became pregnant with my second baby, I knew the move was even more important to keep my family intact.

I was an assistant professor at the medical college for a while but soon quit, though, because the pay was low and the job was stressful. Also, again, the job left me no time to spend with my kids. I threw myself into volunteering and giving back to our new community.

> *"It is health that is real wealth and not pieces of gold and silver."*
> *- Gandhi*

Through this, I made friends and felt good about helping others.

Then, after using their supplements and products for three years, I found my perfect career when I attended USANA Health Sciences, Inc.'s convention. Many people there spoke to the audience about how to help ordinary people realize their dreams. I was impressed by the amount of young, passionate people who were there to learn.

Scientist and founder, Dr. Myron Wentz shared the quality and science behind the products. I love Dr. Wentz's vision, "I dream of a world free from pain and suffering. I dream of a world free from disease. The USANA family will be the healthiest family on Earth. Share my vision. Love life and live it to its fullest in happiness and health." I learned how to get optimal nutrition, about life enhancement both mentally and physically, and about the connection between eating correctly and the prevention of degenerative diseases.

Now, I represent these high-quality products, and my medical background gives me credibility in the world of health. I love having over 3,000 clients around the world, some of whom work with me. I no longer have a boss: I am the boss! I feel blessed to work for such a good company. I appreciate USANA's mission and everything my job brought to me, from the wealth to the good health. Even the challenges over the years were worth it, because they aided my self-development.

When I was little, I spent five years living with my grandmother in the countryside in China. I was a two-year-old when I was sent there, because my parents were too busy with work, and because we lived in a tiny brick home. My grand-mother's house had no electricity or plumbing. We used kerosene lamps, cooked the fish and crabs we caught over fire-wood, and washed our clothes in the stream behind the house. We had no television or radio, so I listened to a lot of stories and loved to star gaze at night, looking up at the big beautiful sky. My grandmother would tell me about her dreams and say that, "someday we will live in a house with an upstairs and a down-stairs. We will have electricity and telephone." She had clear goals for our future. Now my husband and I own more than one beautiful home, and they all have more than one floor and multiple electronic conveniences. I wish my grandmother could see how far I've come.

What about your own life goals and dreams? Examine your life. Think about what you would like to achieve. What step would you need to take to make your dreams a reality? Start making moves, daily, in the direction of your dreams. It was my dream to spend time with my children, earning a high income from home, enjoying life, and living it to its fullest in happiness and health. Now I am experiencing that dream come true!

I am so proud to have a wall in our home covered in awards, plaques, and ribbons from the successes of my family. My older son was North East Junior Golf Tour Champion 2010. Recently, my little boy won a high honor at the Pittsburgh Piano Teachers Association 2011 Duet Competition. Our children's educations are our best investment. You need time, money to provide for them, and most of all, love. Give your kids dreams and spaces to develop.

I love to golf with my two sons, salsa dance, and do Jazzercise. In fact, my whole family is benefiting from good health with a balanced diet, high quality supplements, and exercise. My mom recently called me from China to tell me she climbed 3,660 meters up a mountain without shortness of breath. My mother is 78 years old! I just received her letter with pictures and other proof of her accomplishments. It detailed all the places she went in fifteen days, while she realized her dream of visiting her elderly uncle.

No matter your situation or what may have happened to you over the years, you have things to be thankful for in your life. The more connected you stay to what you are thankful for, the more your life can move toward your passions.

One of my passions is giving back. It is important that my children see me volunteering, helping people change to a healthier lifestyle, and working with the Children's Hunger Fund. If we expect our kids to be extraordinary in the future, we need to set a good example!

Beverly Sills says, "There are no shortcuts to any place worth going." Envision your dreams. Imagine traveling, where you will live, who you will be with, and what you will accomplish in your life. Live a healthy lifestyle and give back to society. Focus on the fulfillment of your goals and take positive action today.

Mary Beth Chapman, founder of showHOPE and wife of singer Steven Curtis Chapman, said, "Let's not waste one minute [by] not championing the cause of the orphans, the hungry, the hurting. Get involved in the work of Children's Hunger Fund; it's amazing work." Queeney supports the charity 501(c)3 nonprofit organization Children's Hunger Fund. Find out more at www.chfus.org.

Chapter 11

Randy Swanson

RANDY SWANSON

Not many people have visited the North Pole because of the extremely cold temperatures (as low as ⁻65°F). Randy Swanson, a mechanic from Grand Rapids, Michigan, achieved the impressive expedition goal of traveling by foot 200 miles to the North Pole in 16 days.

During a trip to Canada's Northwest Territory, I ran into a man named Paul Shurke, who told me about his upcoming trip to the North Pole. I had never met anyone who wanted to go, but as soon as I heard it, something inside me said, "That's for you!"

Before going, I needed to prepare. You must learn to live in the cold, though you can't do much to prepare for the freezing temperatures.

Endurance is majorly important, and from that standpoint, I wasn't ready. I needed to get myself into peak physical condition. Cross training was important: running 35 miles a week, hiking, swimming, weight training, and biking. I would put on a backpack that weighed 65 pounds, harness a 25-pound truck tire to my backpack, and roam the streets of my town, going anywhere from 5 to 15 miles.

I put a lot of time and effort into cross-country skiing, improving my skills and gaining endurance, because that would be my main mode of transportation on the trip. Also, as a team, we took a trip to do training exercises with the dogs and the sleds, spending most of those 10-hour-days trudging through snow.

At the end of that trip, the guides tested our mental fortitude by taking us to "the refrigerator of the nation" lake in Ely, Minnesota. On cue — and with our backpacks on — we had to ski into water in a hole cut into the icy lake. Then we had to get out without assistance. Why? It prepared us for a moment which almost all of us would experience on the North Pole trip: falling through ice and into the cold Arctic Ocean with air temperature between ⁻15 and ⁻65 degrees.

Finally, we were ready to brave the Arctic. We allotted enough food for us and the dogs for the trip so we had to make the 200-mile trek to the Pole in time or risk running out of food and canceling the trip.

Eleven of us made the trip: ten Americans and one Irishman. One woman was on the trip. Two of the trekkers were experienced in this type of venture, and the rest of us were amateur explorers or outdoorsy people.

People have asked me why I went to the North Pole, and I always tell them, "I didn't know any better." I don't think any of us really understood what we were going to go through.

When we had flown as close to the North Pole as a commercial flight would take us in Canada, we flew another 600 miles on a chartered aircraft and were dropped off at 88 degrees latitude. The plane was flown by an experienced bush pilot who knows exactly where to land and can read the ice to know when it's safe to land.

Once we arrived, our adrenaline surged. Immediately, everyone started throwing our equipment out the door and rushing off the plane. We couldn't stay on the plane too long or the ice might crack. Engines weren't cut off for fear that they wouldn't be able to restart. The people, the dogs, and our equipment had to get out of the planes as fast as possible, so they practically threw us out!

It was a strange feeling, standing there on the ice with the dogs and our equipment just watching the plane fly away. I couldn't help thinking, "Wow. Here we are. This is really happening. There's no turning back." In every direction you look, you see nothing but ice. You can't hear a single sound. Boy, you feel all alone.

The moment didn't last long, though, because the temperatures dictate that you move. You can't travel north as a crow flies. You are actually traveling on the Arctic Ocean – you're not on land anymore. Like the polar bears do, you navigate the ice flows of the 5-million-square-mile Arctic Ocean attempting to reach the North Pole in as straight a line as possible. But on your way, obstacles such as open water or ice that is too thin to support your body weight interrupt your course. The key is to find a way around those open leagues of water and take as direct a path as possible to the North Pole.

In total, we had about 2,000 pounds of supplies, including four tents and two meals a day for each person and dog, and each member was carrying a heavy pack. Our only heat source was two stoves.

We had to consume as many calories as possible because we were burning over 6,000 calories a day due to the effort expended. Keeping up endurance was paramount. The other necessity was staying warm, which also requires heavy caloric intake.

My experience with food on the trek through the North Pole was the same as my experience with food when I went mountain climbing. While you would think that by day's end I'd be ravished and could eat a horse, something happened physically that made me lose my appetite. It was challenging, too, because the food didn't actually taste good. The 6,000 calories we were choking down every day consisted of pasta, and a pound of butter: all fatty and full of carbs. It kept us alive, but it wasn't a four-star meal. You had to force yourself to eat.

> *"Life is either a great adventure or nothing."*
> *– Helen Keller*

We were traveling between eight and twelve hours a day. The first day was over before we realized it. We set up our tents and got in our ⁻40-degree sleeping bags. The first night, lying in my sleeping bag brought more new experiences for me. As we exhaled, moisture gathered on the sleeping bags and immediately froze because of the cold temperatures. Then as we breathed in, the ice melted, and water dripped down on our faces. It made for a soggy night's sleep.

Also, moisture collected on the inside of the tent and turned to ice. Every time the wind would blow, it would shake the ice loose from the tent. It was literally snowing inside the tent.

We made it through the first night and woke up the next morning to find that our boots were covered in and full of snow or ice. Our clothing was wet. To start out the second day like that was quite a shock. As I was getting dressed that morning, I started wondering what I had gotten myself into.

You might think everyone brought several changes of clothing, but surprisingly, we wore the same clothes over and over again. The only additional clothing we had was for layering. In spite of the cold temperatures, because you're exerting so much energy during the day while you're traveling, you get warm. The heavier clothing must be put on when you stop moving or you quickly lose the body heat that was created while you traveled.

During the Minnesota training, we learned how to use a sextant, noting the position of the stars, using some log rhythmic calculations, and plotting it on a chart the way they did in 1909. We also brought a GPS as backup. The sextant was soon abandoned because of the extreme conditions. We were so tired and cold. While sometimes we used shadows and the direction of the wind to guide us, the GPS was simply much easier and more reliable than other methods.

Frostbite was a big concern and quite a learning curve for me. One thing I regret is that we really weren't given adequate training to help us prepare for and deal with frostbite. I was shocked by how quickly it could occur. Without gloves on, you had about three seconds before the cold became unbearable, and you needed to put them back on. We had to take our gloves off often to untangle the dogs from their harnesses or to make equipment adjustments, so we had to do it quickly.

In fact, you could stand still for about three minutes without exercising before you would lose all of your body heat. Then once you started up again, it would take about 30 minutes of hard work to get your heart pumping and produce the heat to reach your extremities. Of course, the toes, nose, ears, and fingers are the last places to receive the blood flow, so those are the first places that are susceptible to frostbite.

We all noticed frostbite on our extremities after the first two or three days. Most of it was superficial, and we learned how to deal with it. Later on in the trip, one person got severe frostbite on his hands and feet, though.

I had several areas of superficial frostbite. About the top ½ inch of one of my thumbs got frostbitten pretty badly. First, it turned yellow, then it turned all black, and then the skin started feeling like a piece of wood or cardboard. When I got home, I didn't need to have it treated. The old skin blistered away, and the new skin underneath was healthy.

Others didn't fare as well. As he marched along on the trail, Dave started to fall behind. He was losing energy and didn't look good. He made it to the end of day five when we set up camp. At that point, he already had severe frostbite and decided that he wanted to be airlifted home, which I should mention costs a minimum of sixty thousand dollars. If you're going to do that, you're not doing it for mere blisters. It has to be something serious.

Our guide, Paul Shurke, encouraged Dave to continue on with the team. If Dave couldn't continue, the entire group might have to abort the trip, so Paul wanted him to gut it out.

Dave must have had a lot of mixed emotions. I'm sure he was scared. Losing your fingers and toes is a possibility that goes through your mind. You don't want to let the team down or go home without accomplishing what you started out for. Emotions tug at you from different directions, making a decision hard.

Just because you request to be airlifted home, there's no guarantee that they can come get you. The weather has to cooperate. Also, they have to be able to land on the ice at your position. Even if you need a rescue, if those two things don't line up, it might not happen.

Dave was in a lot of pain, but we managed to move forward the next day. Later that day on the trail, he collapsed about 60 yards or so ahead of me. I caught up to him and knew immediately by looking in his eyes that he was in trouble. We summoned Paul, who was out front. I thought we'd have to set up camp, get Dave in a sleeping bag in the tent, and get him warm, so I was surprised when Paul told us, "To stop is to die." We had no option but to move forward and try to warm Dave from the inside out through movement.

With that, we took Dave's backpack off of him so he had no load. We walked slowly, arm-in-arm for the next three hours. The whole time I talked to him. I asked him questions to keep him coherent and to be sure he wasn't losing it mentally from the frostbite and fatigue. He ended up making it through that day.

Back at camp, we fed him some hot soup, put him to bed early in a sleeping bag, and kept an eye on him. The next morning, he was quite a bit better. Dave made it through the trip, although not without suffering. His hands were so frostbitten that he needed help dressing and feeding himself the remainder of the trip.

Another friend, Alan — the first Irishman to walk to the North Pole — sustained an injury when he was crossing a "pressure ridge" in the dog sleds. Because the Arctic Ocean is five million square miles of ice flows, not all solid ice or cold open water, the wind and temperature can change the "landscape." As the wind blows, huge sheets of ice, sometimes 100 miles wide, slam into each other, creating these pressure ridges. The ice rises above the surface and refreezes. Pressure ridges can become huge mountains of hard, sharp ice chunks, some as high as 30 feet tall.

Crossing pressure ridges becomes quite a scene. To figure out the best way to go over them, we usually had to stop. The minute you stop, though, the dogs start getting antsy. They want to pull all day long. Their energy gets pent up, so by the time you decide to go, the dogs are full of adrenaline and going nuts. It is dangerous to have the dogs react this way while you are dealing with pressure ridges. Navigating the sleds and the people through the ice without breaking the sleds or hurting yourself or the dogs is quite a challenge. While we were navigating a pressure ridge, the sled hit the ice, which shifted, slamming Alan's leg between the sled and a huge chunk of ice.

By evening, his leg had swollen to about twice its original size and was completely black.

Alan basically dealt with it for the remainder of the trip. There was no treatment given to his leg. He just let nature take its course and fortunately for him, it healed on its own.

Another pressure ridge obstacle happened when we punctured one of our fuel canisters for cooking, losing our fuel. That was a pivotal moment in the trip because it affects more than cooking. Food is prepared and eaten in the kitchen tent, which is big enough for everyone to gather inside. If you can leave the stoves on for maybe twenty minutes or longer after cooking, it gives you a chance to dry out all of your wet clothing. This luxury was given up because losing that fuel put us on minimum rations;

"When one man for whatever reason has the opportunity to lead an extraordinary life, he has no right to keep it to himself."
- Jacques Cousteau

we could no longer afford to use it for heat. Having it strictly for cooking our food made a big impact on comfort – or lack of it – for the remainder of the trip.

The trip required an "all-for-one and one-for-all" attitude right from the beginning. We needed each other and knew that our survival depended on cooperation. We needed to have the will to survive.

Being dependent on each other, we tried not to exceed a certain distance between people as we traveled. We couldn't spread too far apart because we could lose each other due to low visibility. It was hard to keep together, though, because no one travels at the same pace. Sometimes, you had to lag behind a little and wait for the guy behind you. Yet, you're being driven to move faster by how cold you are. And some of us were cross-country skiing while the other four were working the sleds. The skiers couldn't travel at the same pace as the sled drivers, so someone was always waiting on someone else, making sure that everyone made it, even if we were a little colder for it.

I started out skiing and got very frustrated with it because the terrain wasn't smooth, so the skis were constantly sliding out to the side, and it took up a great deal of energy. Some of those who started off sledding found that it wasn't for them, because it was very physical, and the sleds were constantly tipping over. Working the dogs and keeping them in check took a great deal of energy.

People envision that you're just sitting on the back of the sled, and the dogs are pulling you along, zipping over the ice; however, you are actually running beside the sled 90% of the time. It's not very fast. Sometimes hanging onto the back of the sled while you were running was an option. The dogs would move faster than you could typically run, though, so you were almost being pulled along by the sleds part of the time. It's like holding onto a bike seat while running next to a moving bicycle.

We had to be very careful about how much energy the dogs expended. They are bred to pull, and they love to pull, so that's what they want to do to all day long. Unfortunately, if you let them, they'll run themselves into the ground and then crash out from exhaustion and you won't get them to move for three days. You can't let it get to that point because, if the dogs stop for three days, the trip is over. Our provisions wouldn't allow for it.

At one point in the trip, I actually didn't think we were going to reach the pole. In fact, it wasn't until day 10, when we were about 25 miles from our goal, that I was optimistic that we'd get there. Before that, we weren't making the progress that we wanted to and had run into problems with injuries that slowed us down.

An open lead of water – a pathway that isn't frozen over – caused us to travel four miles to the west. That cost us a lot of time. We were also floating one mile per day south, so if we traveled ten miles, we actually only made it nine miles north. A similar trip about two years before ours was actually aborted because they were floating thirteen miles south a day.

The last day was surreal. I don't know how much of it was in our heads or how much was reality, but the last day just fell into place for us. The wind had died down and it made for a nice day of travel. Everything seemed prettier that day. In the ice and in the water, we saw many different shades of white and blue. Some breathtaking ice formations were seen. It was just a beautiful day. Everything worked, and it seemed that we were destined to get there.

A mile out from the pole, we decided to let Corky Peterson, the oldest member of our group (a 69-year-old from Minnesota) lead us the rest of the way to the North Pole. What's strange is that when you get to the North Pole, it kind of looks like where you started: there is nothing there. It's all open ice. The only way you know you're there is the GPS. Once you hit that 90 degree mark, you have reached it. Of course, you can't rely on a compass because they don't work once you get that far north. When we finally got there, it was really sweet – lots of hugs and celebration.

On the day we arrived at the pole, we only spent a little bit of time there. A lot of us took a ceremonial "walk around the world" where we crossed all the lines of longitude, literally walking around the world in less than half a minute. Soon, we headed to set up camp.

The next day was when what we had accomplished hit me. We were proud and grateful that Mother Nature allowed us to get there. By then, our team had a real camaraderie, so the last day was emotional and bittersweet. Our accomplishment was humbling.

When you're standing on the top of the world, you recognize your insignificance as a human. You are there by the grace of God. You know you can be swallowed up in a second by Mother Nature. Being there makes you appreciate what you have. It gives you a sense of what you're made of, and it teaches you a lot about yourself.

Go for your dreams. It doesn't have to be the North Pole. Any accomplishment can be your North Pole. This is why we have ordinary people and an extraordinary planet, just like the name of this radio show and book. If you had known me in 1995, and I told you I would end up at the North Pole, you'd never believe me. Then, I was nothing but ordinary. I guess the lesson is that ordinary people *can* do extraordinary things!

Randy Swanson raises money for Gilda's Club, which has created welcoming communities of free support for everyone living with cancer, along with their families and friends. Their innovative program is an essential complement to medical care, providing networking and support groups, workshops, education, and social activities. To learn more, go to www.gildasclub.org.

Chapter 12

Mary K. Hoodhood

MARY K. HOODHOOD

Think about how you feel when your stomach starts rumbling. It's beyond needing a snack . . . you need a meal. You walk to your refrigerator, grab something out of your garden, or place an order at a restaurant. Some children don't have these options. Mary K. Hoodhood from Grand Rapids, Michigan, is the founder of Kids' Food Basket. She received the Presidential Citizen's Medal because the organization she founded feeds over 3,000 hungry American children daily.

My favorite thing to talk about is childhood hunger. Any opportunity I have, I make people aware that children around us are going to bed hungry. I'm glad to about talk it. We started feeding kids in November of 2001 and haven't stopped yet.

MaryAnn Prisichenko, a principal in Grand Rapids, made me aware of children going hungry right here in Michigan. When she caught her students digging through a trash can, she asked what they were doing. They said they were looking for food. She began talking to school administrators, teachers, and school nurses, but they responded that, in fact, a lot of kids had self-reported that they don't eat at home.

That November, we started feeding 125 kids a sack supper, and the need has risen over the years. Unbelievably, today we are feeding over 3,700 kids every weekday!

The rise in the number of hungry children coincided with the economic meltdown. Currently, we work with schools in Michigan: Grand Rapids, Wyoming, and Kelloggsville. This area experienced a trickle-down effect from the car industry because the big GM Manufacturing Plants closed, and then the car parts industry suffered when Ford stopped making as many cars here. Soon it seemed that everyone was being laid off, which always means less food on people's tables.

The need has certainly been greater because of the economy; however, many children were in need before the economy tanked. Poverty is common here. Our research has shown that a lot of two-parent households where both are only making minimum wage live here, and such a tight budget can't stretch to feed their families.

The districts knew that the kids needed meals, yet they didn't know the extent of the problem. The schools were feeding the kids breakfast and lunch already through the "reduced lunch programs." But they were unaware that when the children went home, they were actually being fed very little, if at all.

MaryAnn's students were five-year-old kids and younger, in preschool, kindergarten, and first grade, searching for something that they could eat for dinner. It is such an early age to have to look for food and come up empty.

Through Kids' Food Basket, we also researched what the lack of food and calories does to these kids. We found that nutritional deficiency can hinder their brain growth and development.

All the kids we feed at Kids' Food Basket are under 12 years old. We are in 27 schools, and have 13 schools on our waiting list. We are doing a really good job, but we still have a ways to go.

I was working at a soup kitchen when I founded Kids' Food Basket. I'm a Volunteer Coordinator by profession. Sadly, I know first-hand that when you have a good idea, a lot of times the stumbling block is lack of manpower. That wasn't a problem for Kids' Food Basket, however, because I had volunteers ready to secure food, assemble sack suppers, and deliver the meals.

Because of my experience coordinating a Meals-on-Wheels program, I knew how to feed people, so I could easily coordinate volunteers and provide access to food.

Also, about four months before I started Kids' Food Basket, my boss had given me an article about a woman in Los Angeles who wanted to do something about children who went hungry during the summer. She had a van and a bunch of food and would drive around with a bullhorn, playing music. Like children hurrying to meet an ice cream truck on a hot day, the kids came running out of their houses to get the nutritious food.

Due to this, I had already had an image of childhood hunger in mind. When we started feeding the kids, we were unaware of the number of kids at risk. With more research, we identified kids who were hungry and also living below the poverty level. We decided to form a nonprofit agency with a mission to feed them. What we didn't know was that so many would need to get meals.

It's amazing to watch the growth. Fortunately, I was in a position to work with many volunteers and a wonderful, dedicated executive director to make this happen. As I look back, I realize it was a big undertaking. I knew that with the support of the tenacious volunteers and community, we could do it for the children.

The reason we have such a big waiting list –13 schools – and why we have been so successful in feeding kids is because we're calculated in our growth. We don't say, "Okay, we think there are 5,000 kids, let's go feed them all." After all, you must have access to food, you have to have enough volunteers, and you have to have the money to buy the food you need.

About eight months ago, we moved to a new location, which solved our previous problems with space and storage. Being so calculated in our growth, like making sure that we could do the move and still feed the children, truly has been the key to our success.

It's overwhelming to hear the extreme need that exists, but that's what drives us. And the food doesn't go unappreciated. We note the attitude of the little kids who are receiving the food. They truly are thankful.

Children who are used to not having food behave differently from a child who is used to eating regularly. One little girl started receiving the sack supper right after Christmas. The first day that she got her meal, the teacher gave it to her, and she took it home. The next morning, she had part of it with her at school. The teacher said, "What happened? Didn't you like the food?" The girl explained that she was saving it because she didn't know if she was going to get another sack supper the next day.

Another kid who receives the meals is 10 years old; his mother has the mental capacity of a 12-year-old. The social workers who work with him were using the sack supper as a good example of what a nutritious meal looks like. They were able to educate his mother on what is healthy to feed her child.

We hear tons of stories about the children who we provide food for throughout the week. We get a lot of positive feedback. Some of the families are immigrants living in apartments near the schools, who come from places like Bosnia and Somalia. Without their sack suppers, they wouldn't eat an evening meal. Others have working single moms who go to work right after their kids come home from school, and our program ensures that the children receive a nutritious meal that evening.

One time, the teacher caught a girl stealing an extra sack supper, which explained why they were always one short. When the teacher asked the student why she took it, the child said it was to feed her little sister. After hearing stories like this, we became aware of younger kids at home who obviously have the same need. We send an extra sack supper home with them for siblings.

I am so proud that we give the kids a meat sandwich, a healthy snack, and a fruit and vegetable every day. Also, we provide a 100% fruit juice drink. Our menu is very nutritious; we include all five food groups.

On a personal note, I was in an automobile accident in 1980. As a result of a spinal cord injury, I'm a quadriplegic. Michigan is a "no fault" state so I have a personal care attendant to assist me with the activities of daily living. I need to be driven everywhere, and they help me with eating and with all my basic care needs.

When I was first injured, I was told that if I got a job they would not provide a personal care attendant to assist me while on the job. They thought the attendant would be doing the entire job for me. However, I demonstrated that I was fully capable. I went back to school and earned a master's degree in social work. I showed the state that I could run meetings, coordinate programs, and fulfill all the qualifications of my job.

I have been married to my husband, Jeff, for thirty years. I recall when I woke up after the accident, my first thought was,

"Jeff will never leave me." I knew in my heart that even though we were not yet married, he would be by my side. He says with a grin that he knew he, "couldn't let this one get away." Even though others were concerned that caring for me would take a toll on our relationship, we have proven how strong our love is for each other.

Obviously, I would have every excuse to just lay back and take it easy, but that has never been something I could do. Like everybody else, though, sometimes I don't feel well, and I tell my doctor that "this disability gets in the way of my life!"

I was honored at the White House by none other than President Barack Obama. Bridget Clark Whitney, our Executive Director, nominated me to receive the Presidential Citizen's Medal. The President himself narrowed it down to 13 people from the United States who he wanted to honor, out of 6,000 applicants. On August 4, 2010, my husband and I went to the White House, and it was just beautiful. It was overwhelming and surreal. When you go to the White House, you can just smell the history there. Beautiful paintings of the presidents and the first ladies hang on the walls. The Secret Service was everywhere, and many of them were dressed in military uniforms. It was an absolutely amazing and wonderful experience. The event was even more special to me because it meant that people *nationally* were learning about childhood hunger and Kids' Food Basket.

Meeting President Obama was an unbelievable experience. He's charming and engaging, and it was such an honor to be there. I was amazed by how down-to-Earth he seemed. It was actually his birthday that day, so he was going directly from the event to his former home in Chicago. He said, "I can't wait to sleep in my own bed." It was such a normal thing to say.

The White House was conscientious of the fact that I couldn't reach for or hold the award so they let my husband come up to the front and accept the honor with me. When the President presented me with the award, I accepted it, "on behalf of all the wonderful people who day-in and day-out feed our kids."

In 2010, we were honored at the state level, and I was delighted. The Kids' Food Basket was named the Outstanding Volunteer Management Program of Michigan. We utilize 145 volunteers a day, so we are certainly volunteer-driven! What's interesting is that 25% of our volunteers are under 18 years of age. It's a great opportunity for kids to give back to the community. Anybody over 5 years old can volunteer. The child volunteers may even be helping somebody they know. Some of the child volunteers also receive a sack supper at their school. So not only are they getting a healthy dinner, they are also learning to give back to the community.

Some people think that programs like ours are just Band-aids, that we aren't getting to the heart of the problem by feeding other people's kids. But when the problem is poverty, the key is

> *"Disability is a matter of perception. If you can do just one thing well, you're needed by someone."*
> *-Martina Navratilova*

to provide the means for the next generation to rise above it. By getting a healthy meal, children will be able to learn better, both because their brains will develop better and because that rumble in their stomachs won't be distracting them from their education. With an education, these kids have the opportunity for better jobs, college, scholarships, and a whole world of mental development that will make them able to provide for themselves, and hopefully to provide for their own children.

Of course, this would make Kids' Food Basket obsolete, and frankly, I would love to be out of business. But, right now, we are definitely needed. It only costs one dollar to feed a child that meal, and it is worth a buck to know that the children are getting fed.

People in the community are starting to recognize me, usually with a smile, and hopefully with a thought about doing something for the hungry children. Sometimes, I receive other honors, like the one from the *Grand Rapids Business Journal*. I was named one of the Fifty Most Influential Women in West Michigan. I thought this was remarkable because I didn't know I was "influential." It's still funny to me that people recognize me, but I don't mind it, as long as I am influencing them to help the children.

We have a vision to feed all the hungry children in the greater Grand Rapids area in the next three years. That means that our target is to feed around 5,000 children a day.

In every elementary school we serve, about 100 children, on average, are at risk of not receiving an evening meal. Our collaborating schools are those with 80% of the kids living at or below the poverty level. We need volunteers, financial help, and, as always, access to good, nutritious food.

Our Expansion Task Force intends to mentor other cities to create similar programs. From as far away as Hawaii, Chattanooga and New York City, multiple requests have come in, asking for information on how they can model our program. We have heard the same request from many other cities, all over the United States. Because of the rise in interest in our program, we are also working on a manual so people can easily replicate what we do.

I have been blessed with an even temper, coping skills, and a great support network. When I'm working with KFB, people look at me in my wheelchair and think one of two things, either "Mary K. does a lot even though she is disabled, so I can do my part," or simply, "Boy . . . she needs a lot of help." Either way, whatever motivates people, I don't care. But know this: if I can do what I've done, everybody can do it!

Instead of looking at the litany of things I can't do, I always focus on what I can do for kids we serve. It would be a sin if I didn't do it, because I can.

I am always motivated to contact a person or company and tell them about what Kids' Food Basket needs. I know that it will directly impact the children we feed. I would love it if everyone who reads this book would, in the next week, tell five people about Kids' Food Basket and ask those five people to get involved in some way. I always say, "Less talk and more action. Now, let's go make a sandwich, and feed a kid!"

Dear KFB,

Thank you for the amazing sock suppers. I really like the soft sandwich. They help me to have a fresh mind. I wish I had a hill of sock suppers! I feel good that I had a treash sandwich!

Sincerely,
Jennifer

Author's Note

Thank you for joining us on this journey into the fascinating lives of the people inside the pages of this book. Ray Leonard was a great partner throughout the book writing process. As an interviewee on Ray's show, myself, I am humbled to be in such incredible company. As the author, I feel blessed to have had the opportunity to connect with these lovely people.

Throughout the process, many of my heroes in this book became close friends of mine. I was delighted to learn that Clarel Radicella did survive to make it to her beautiful daughter's wedding. I was deeply saddened to learn of Clarel's passing; yet, I knew that her legacy would live on through this book and her children. It was gratifying when Randy Swanson, who traveled to the North Pole said, "I could tell that you grasped the experience behind the words." I was able to chat with Mary K. Hoodhood as Ray Leonard and I attended a Kid's Food Basket fundraiser that made over $40,000 for the cause; I also interviewed Mary K. and her husband Jeff on video about their incredible love story. These people allowed us into their hearts and lives for this book and for that I am thankful.

If you or someone you know is an ordinary person that has an extraordinary life story to tell the world, please go to kmr-media.com and share it with Ray Leonard. Select stories will be chosen for future radio interviews and could possibly be included in future Ordinary People Extraordinary Planet books.

We are committed to helping the causes in this book. 25% of the net profits from the sales of this book will be divided amongst the charities inside when we hit the 100,000 books sold benchmark. Please help the causes — from cancer awareness to hungry and homeless children — by spreading the word about this book to organizations, book clubs, schools, and friends. Together as a global community, we can make a profound difference in the lives of others!

108

About the Author

Dr. Shellie Hipsky's career includes teaching students from kindergarten to the doctoral level in the United States as well as in Rome, Italy. She is a graduate of Duquesne University's IDPEL doctoral program in educational leadership and has presented at an international conference on educational leadership at the University of Oxford in Oxford, England. The research methodology she created, called the "Pre-Conceptual Map," was taught in a Harvard University Research Methods course. This former special education teacher and assistant principal has published over one hundred articles. Hipsky's authored books include *The Drama Discovery Curriculum, Arts Alive,* and *Differentiating Literacy and Language Arts Strategies for the Elementary Classroom.* Her latest book was *Mentoring Magic: Pick the Card for Your Success* (mentoringmagic.net), which is a powerful tool for students around the globe to network and find, form, and sustain a mentoring relationship. She is a frequently requested speaker by educational organizations, corporations, schools, conferences and talk shows on differentiated instruction, mentoring, and powerfully inspirational messages. She can be booked for speaking and media appearances through **www.shelliehipsky.com**, or send her an email at **contact@shelliehipsky.com**. Dr. Hipsky educates, entertains, and inspires globally.